SOLANO COMMUNITY COLLEGE

D0941319

ARSHILE GORKY

Ethel K. Schwabacher:

*Portrait by
Gjon Mili, 1946*

ARSHILE GORKY

With a Preface by

Lloyd Goodrich

and an Introduction by

Meyer Schapiro

Published for the

Whitney Museum of American Art

by The Macmillan Company

New York, 1957

© Whitney Museum of American Art 1957

All rights reserved—no part of this book may
be reproduced in any form without permission
in writing from the publisher, except by a
reviewer who wishes to quote brief passages
in connection with a review written for inclusion
in magazine or newspaper.

First Printing

Printed in the United States of America

Designed by Peter Oldenburg

Library of Congress catalog card number: 57–12946

6-16-58

8
ND
237
G613
S36

VALLEJO JUNIOR COLLEGE LIBRARY

ND
237
G613
S36

7713

To Wolf, Brenda and Chris

Contents

This book is that rare thing, a record of an artist by another artist who not only understands him completely but has the gift of expressing that understanding in words.

Arshile Gorky was a powerful and tragic figure. The tragedy lay in his life—an idyllic childhood closing in catastrophe, years of poverty and struggle in a new world, brief recognition, then an untimely death. But in his art, with its instinctual power and passion, its sensuous richness, and its wealth of poetic imagery, he triumphed over personal misfortune, and made a major contribution to modern painting. *Preface*

Ethel Schwabacher, herself a gifted, sensitive and highly individual painter, met Gorky in 1928. From the first she was deeply impressed by his work, particularly by the strength of his drawing. After an interval of several years abroad, she began studying with him in 1934. He no longer had regular classes, and she and her friend Mina Metzger were among a few pupils he taught in his studio; for two seasons she worked there three days a week. To his gift as a teacher she pays tribute in this book. His teaching was not confined to the studio: with that passion for great art that was so deep in him, he took his students often to the Metropolitan Museum to study the masters of the past, and to realize the abstract form that underlies representation.

The relation of master and pupil grew into a friendship that lasted the rest of Gorky's life. Mrs. Schwabacher saw him constantly, looked at every picture he painted, visited galleries with him, discussed mutual ideas; and he in turn followed her work, whose intensely personal poetry he admired, and gave her perceptive and stimulating criticism. Since he struggled almost all his life against non-recognition and poverty, she and her husband Wolfgang Schwabacher helped by buying his work and encouraging others to do so. In 1941 they gave the Museum of Modern Art his *Image in Xhorkom*, one of his earliest museum acquisitions. Wolf Schwabacher, with characteristic quiet generosity, assisted him in practical affairs, and in 1946 secured a foundation grant which helped to ease his circumstances.

Ethel Schwabacher first conceived the idea of this book in the spring of 1948. I remember how she and Wolf came to see me about the project, and how valuable it seemed to me—a book on a living American artist, recording at firsthand his art and thought. Gorky himself was delighted

9

with the plan, and that it would be carried out by one who knew him so well, and who was, as he told her, "a poet." He suggested as a model Robert Melville's little volume, *Picasso: Master of the Phantom*. There were preliminary conversations, and Agnes Gorky began to make notes of her husband's ideas and memories. Then came the tragic sequence of events that led to Gorky's suicide in July.

It was appropriate that the memorial exhibition of his work in January 1951 should have been held by the Whitney Museum. The Whitney had exhibited his pictures consistently for years, first in its "Abstract Painting in America" show in 1935, and thereafter in most of its annual shows; and in 1937 it had purchased his *Painting*—his first museum purchase. In organizing the memorial exhibition we had the invaluable help of Mrs. Schwabacher, who in the catalogue text wrote the first biographical and critical study of any length. Her plan for a book was still paramount, and she continued to interview Gorky's friends, to study his pictures, and to gather material of all kinds. In the next few years I had the privilege and pleasure of reading the manuscript in its successive stages, and seeing it grow into a full-scale biography and critique, which combined authentic fact with the most sensitive poetic interpretation. The final editorial stages were in the capable hands of my colleagues John I. H. Baur and Rosalind Irvine, respectively Curator and Associate Curator of the Whitney Museum. The Museum is proud to have played a part in this first book on a major figure in contemporary art, and to have the honor of publishing it.

LLOYD GOODRICH
Associate Director
Whitney Museum of American Art

An artist rarely has the good fortune to be the subject of a study by one who has known him well and has loved his art with as much understanding as the exquisitely sensitive author of this book. She was Gorky's pupil and friend throughout the greater part of his career as a painter.

My own memories and impressions of Gorky are less precise than Ethel Schwabacher's. I met him most often in the museums and galleries fixed in rapt contemplation of pictures with that grave, searching look which was one of the beauties of his face. As some poets are great readers, Gorky—exceptional among painters—was a fervent scrutinizer of paintings. No interesting touch or invention of form escaped his eye. He was equally at home in the Metropolitan Museum and the Museum of Modern Art, keen in discerning what was good in the arts of many ages and styles. He possessed a rare power of artistic recognition founded on a noble concept of art, an aristocratic feeling for quality. He championed the original and the great while most artists around him were contented with much less.

Among the painters in New York, Gorky stood out for years as the masterly apprentice. His career was remarkable as a development from what seemed a servile imitation of other painters to a high orginality. For almost twenty years he produced obviously derived pictures, versions of Cézanne, Picasso, Léger, Miró, Kandinsky and others; and suddenly he flowered as an imaginative artist whom certain admirers class with the very great. That prolonged period of imitation might be regarded as a voluntary and humble discipleship leading to original work; but to those who disparage his last pictures and point to the earlier stage as the measure of a limited, dependent talent, it can be said that never in his fidelity to the masters he loved was Gorky conventional or academic like the conservative and hybrid artists these same critics find it more easy to approve. The painters he followed were his personal discoveries, much like the ancient works copied by the masters of the Renaissance. To be a disciple of Picasso in New York in the 1920's and early '30's was an act of originality and, for a young artist in the solitude of his exceptional taste, an enormous risk.

If we study the young Gorky's "imitations" in themselves, without asking what they copy, we are bound, I think, to recognize, their considerable virtues. In an exhibition of the art of the time they would hold up as works of a true artist: beautiful in color, of an appetizing substance, well constructed, robust, with an air of completeness. Few artists in this country in the 1920's and '30's painted so seriously. To Gorky the great painters of our century were like the old masters, and he gave them his unwavering attention, consulting their pictures with a profoundly searching eye. In imitating Picasso, he wished to possess Picasso's language; his own version was a test of his insight and degree of mastery. In Gorky's picture which resembles the Spaniard's still life with musical instruments in the collection of Mrs. Patrick Hill, shown at the Museum of Modern Art, he was able to use those foreign forms with an amazing sureness. It is hard to believe that this painting was done in New York by an artist who had never been in Paris and knew only the few works of Picasso that had been shown here. We do not find in Gorky's early painting the typical reductions of a more complex or accomplished style that we expect in imitations made at a distance from the home of the original work. There is no trace here of confusion of forms or mark of a previous method of the copyist contaminating the new style—in short, no foreign accent. He belonged then to the School of Paris more surely than many painters living in France. The difference from Picasso lay not so much in the intonation or in the syntax and vocabulary of motifs, which Gorky possessed fully, as in subtler qualities which only an attentive scrutiny will disclose. There is in this imitative phase of Gorky's art a great pride and a great humility, like that of the Renaissance painters and sculptors who thought of the ancients as their true models and did not believe they could surpass them; if their art today seems to us in many respects unclassic, it was not so from a deliberate striving for the new. Gorky was as far from his beloved modern classics in space, as the Renaissance artists were remote from the ancients in time. For years surprising Picassos, Braques and Mirós turned up on 57th Street or at the Museum of Modern Art and in books and magazines, as Roman statuary had emerged from the ground in the 15th century to join the standing objects in the ruins. Until one day, Europe itself was exiled to America and Gorky found himself at last among his own kind. Here his life as an original artist began.

In his career of imitation, he had been attracted by successively younger and perhaps lesser artists, although always highly individual ones. From Cézanne he had gone to Picasso, from Picasso to Miró, and finally, among the surrealists, from Masson and Tanguy to the youngest of all: Matta. The artist he admired now was a brother rather than a father, and a younger brother. In Matta he found for the first time a painter whose language, once mastered, he could use as freely himself. From Matta came the idea of the canvas as a field of prodigious excitement, unloosed energies, bright reds and yellows opposed to cold greys, a new futurism of the organic as well as of mechanical forces. Gorky could draw his own conclusions from Matta's art without waiting for the inventor; he was able to build upon it independently as Braque did upon the forms created jointly by Picasso and himself. The encounter with Matta was, it seems to me, a decisive point in Gorky's liberation from copying.

In the advanced American art of the 1940's one cannot stress too much the importance of the influx of European artists in New York during the war, and most of all the surrealists, in spite of the barrier of language. Gorky had known their work before and his painting had responded already to the imagery of Miró and Picasso's fantasy about primitive bodily forms. But in the war years Gorky accepted the undiscipline of surrealism (which had also its requirements of harmony); and this released in him qualities he had perhaps not suspected in himself before. His painting had been a homage to stable order, deliberation, substance; in his last works how tenuous, loose and scattered are the playful forms! But also how refined the tones and surface, how elegant the calligraphy of the bodiless linear shapes, sometimes to the point of the precious and prolix! In the first pictures he kept the spectator at a distance, as before a high mural which must be seen from afar if its architecture is to be grasped and the full effect of its primary colors enjoyed. Afterwards he is caressing and graceful, inviting us to a close view of secret detail, the vagrant lines and thin washes of mysterious color melting into each other and into the canvas grain. The novelty of his style lies in part in his creation of the atmospheric in an art which had been until then airless and precise. In Miró's painting there is something of this filmy ambience, but it is most often the clear air of Mediterranean landscape or the transparent depth of an ocean or aquarium, the home of floating creatures. Gorky discovered an atmosphere suited for the objects of modern fantasy, primitive, visceral and grotesque, as Corot had created an atmosphere for nostalgic revery, a sweet mythical world that might have been seen directly. Gorky's atmosphere, veiling the hard opaque wall of the canvas, evokes a nocturnal void or the vague, unstable image-space of the day-dreaming mind. But beyond the appeal of the painting as a secretion of symbols or as a track of feeling, Gorky's work has usually the grace of art—it is beautifully made.

Here in exile in New York the surrealists of the Old World found their last original disciple. Gorky, as I said, had been prepared for their visit years before. He had known and loved their vein of revolt and their flair for the instinctual in poetry, painting and wit. In the '30's he had admired Dali both as writer and imagier, in spite of his own high scruples

13

about art. Admitted to the fold, Gorky yielded to the seduction of surrealist poetics, accepting and soliciting others' titles for his works—which as improvisations had no predetermined sense. He once said that he did not wish his pictures to have faces; but he sometimes gave them what are artificial faces, the masks of borrowed allusions, poets' titles. Yet in the best of his last pictures, very beautiful ones like *Agony* and the *Diary of a Seducer,* he seems to us truer to himself than in his most austerely considered early work; at least he was able to realize then in a delicate style an important, perhaps feminine, part of his nature—feelings of love and fragility and despair—for which there had been little place in his art before.

MEYER SCHAPIRO

It occurred to me in the spring of 1948 that I might write a book about Arshile Gorky and thus bring his work, as yet insufficiently known, before the public. The book was to have been done in collaboration with his wife, Agnes Gorky, the plan being to note down his conversation in order "to crystallize thought and action into communicable form."[1] This effort was cut short by Gorky's death in 1948.

Because he was an Armenian, Gorky's conception of facts was typical of the East rather than the West. As his wife later wrote to me, explaining the varying and at times fanciful accounts he gave of his birthplace and of his life in general: "Gorky imbued me with a deep distrust of facts and he constantly felt that people misunderstood each other because they did not listen to what one was trying to say, but to what one said."[2] There is little documentary material about Gorky's life beyond a few letters to his wife and to his sister, Vartoosh Mooradian, to whom he wrote in Armenian. In later years Agnes Gorky took over the responsibility for most of her husband's correspondence with his family and friends. Thus I have relied chiefly on my own insight into Gorky's personality. My friendship with Gorky, which began when I studied with him from 1934 to 1936, continued over a period of fifteen years. From the time I married Wolfgang S. Schwabacher in 1935, my husband served as Gorky's lawyer, and both of us were admirers and purchasers of his work; we were frequently with him during the years when he was in New York and in constant communication with him during the later years which he spent for the most part in Virginia and Connecticut. After Gorky's death his friends were most generous in sharing their knowledge of his life and work with me. This, then, was the reservoir of information on which I drew. When, occasionally, I felt that it would bring Gorky more vividly before the reader, I condensed several hitherto separate insights, experiences or observations into one paragraph. I have traced Gorky's life from the idyllic peace of childhood to the terror and poverty of boyhood, emigration as a youth of fifteen to America (at which point the Armenian, Vosdanig Adoian, took the pseudonym "Gorky"—in Russian "the bitter one"), the struggle to succeed in that land of promise, and, after a short period of renewed happiness in the early years of his marriage, the tragic bitterness, frustration, emotional bankruptcy and illness of the last years, culminating in his suicide at the age of forty-three.

15

When I first knew him Gorky frequently went with his pupils to 57th Street. In the early thirties this street was already the center of the New York art world and perhaps had superseded Paris as the center of the international art world. "Fifty-seventh Street" extended from beyond Lexington Avenue on the east to Sixth Avenue on the west; it really extended down to Alfred Stieglitz' An American Place, at 509 Madison Avenue, and up to Julien Levy's gallery at 59th and Madison; perhaps even farther, to the Wildenstein at 64th Street halfway between Madison and Fifth Avenues.

As we went from one gallery to another, many people turned to look at Gorky. Lean, handsome, shabby, he towered above the crowd. Quite as he has depicted in various self-portraits, his black hair sharply defined the olive-white forms of forehead and cheek; his eyebrows arched well above up-slanted eyes; his long, low-bridged nose curved over his moustache, half concealing his sensuous mouth. His suit was patched with leather at the elbows, the too short sleeves accentuating heavily veined wrists and enormous knobbed hands. There was in him a curious mixture of genius and tramp, poet and clown; he was impressive and grotesque, admirable and pathetic.

At Durand–Ruel, halfway down the block toward Madison Avenue, we found Impressionist masters hung about the velvet walls. Their mood and needs seemed distant then, no longer corresponding to ours. As we tried unsuccessfully to project ourselves into this shimmering, light-filled world, Gorky's thoughts broke out in snatches: "Seductive, yes, they revolted against darkness; there are no lost areas in these paintings as there are in the old masters. . . . The Renaissance discovered chiaroscuro, but the nineteenth century did better, they discovered *light without shadow*." As he studied these forms built of innumerable nuances, an inner ferment exploded into words. "No, it will not do. Form must be unified again—Why break it up?" Reiterating "Why break it up?" Gorky abruptly left the gallery.

Once again on the street, we crossed over to the round "Bus Stop" sign balanced at the curb. Pointing to it, Gorky said his favorite word: "Beautiful." He loved this twentieth-century folk art; from 14th Street to 57th billboards, bus-stop signs, hydrants, cigar-store Indians proclaimed the creative power of the people. He had always believed in the people. As he looked down at the design formed by the cracks on the cement sidewalk he said quietly, "Someday everyone will be his own artist."

But still the inner ferment permitted him no rest. Through his thoughts ran a poem he had copied out with pen on heavy paper:[3]

"So many voices that were calculated even when the speakers smiled had disgusted my ears with hearing.

16

"Over the two Quotidian cobbles, my feet were dragging weighted miles lined with a shadow which as yet had no thickness. Ill the trees were in gallows wood and they were innumerable in the forest of repression with its leaden foliage so thick that, from dawn to dusk and from dusk to dawn one did not dare to imagine that some day, beyond the horizon and beyond habit, there would burst a scene all sulphur and love."

II Arshile Gorky, born in Armenia and coming to America at the age of sixteen, liked to think of himself as part of a Caucasian heritage which retained elements of ancient Sumerian culture. Lake Van, where he lived as a child, had been the center of an Armenian civilization which had celebrated schools of calligraphy and illuminated manuscripts. Raised in the mountains of northern Armenia and the Caucasus, of peasant ancestry on his father's side and a long line of priests on his mother's, Gorky was a man of great physical vigor and creative passion.

Reflecting these qualities, his works were powerful, vital, sensuously rich; his brush had the something which is the birthright of a born painter. He relied upon instinct; he felt rather than reasoned. In his frequent use of metaphor and magic symbolism, dream-world images and animism, distortion and arbitrary color, he was a mythic or intuitive rather than a logical creator. Driven by an insatiable desire to apprehend form and what he termed the "invisible relations and phenomena of this modern time,"[4] he had the courage to stand on the burning ground of the present.

His mind blazed with a fiery river of ever-varying images. His quest was to embody the soul of the image in form. Into his imagery he distilled the experiences of a poet, a poet-in-paint whose range extended from an intuitive, lyrical poetry of nature to a tragic, daemonic poetry of human emotion. It might be said of him that he was the Ingres of the unconscious. He recovered latent images from the unconscious world and incorporated them in a space which he himself had created and in relationships which he had determined. This tapping of the unconscious involved chance, and a certain degree of automatism was used to obtain it; but this chance invariably flowered into choice.

Self-taught, he learned by doing, and by lifelong, passionate absorption in the art of the past and present, studying the works of the museums, the works of living masters and the works of nature with equal intensity. To him a great painter was a masterpiece of nature which every other painter must study. He set himself to learn the methods of the masters, assuming that there were technical means which remain constant. His work evokes the realities and nuances not only of nature, but of the one unchanging element in civilization—art. In the realm of art he wandered

17

freely and loved much. He loved to isolate part of a picture and study it for itself, applying the principle of *pars pro toto* by which every part of the whole is the whole itself and contains its significance. Freed from the weight of emotion aroused by the total effect of a work, he drew from its parts for his creative purposes as freely as from the parts of nature. His own richly sensuous nature transformed all that he took from art into something which had the integrity of the personal plastic creation. Saturated with reminiscences, he transmitted them in his own terms, and we are warmed unforgettably by his store of energy and heat. His aim at first was not so much to make something totally new as to eliminate the obsolete solutions of his predecessors; by combining two or more elements, to produce not new elements but new compounds.

He experimented endlessly, using the wide range of ideologies and techniques offered by his understanding of other art. He tended to push experiments to extremes: from the extreme of abundance, shown in rich substance, paint built up in layer upon layer until it resembled polychromed bas-relief, to the extreme of poverty, shown in thin painting, where the canvas was left bare in large areas, suggesting asceticism. He explored the extremes of blackness and whiteness, of barbaric color and grisaille, of largeness and the precise minutiae of particulars, of the tragic and the lyric.

Creating variations on a theme, he frequently did a succession of paintings on the same subject. The mood and treatment changed radically in each version in accordance with the period in which it was worked; but the themes, which sprang from the deep of his own personality and rewrote the experience of his childhood, remained the same. They were autobiographical; his art, paradoxically, was impersonal.

As he matured, the elements derived from other art were lost in growing independence. His late works achieved the freedom of great knowledge. They were entirely personal, prodigal in original ideas, and filled with a superb creative vitality. The wealth of invention shown in subtle metamorphoses of forms and images is fantastic. These works revealed him in full possession of his means, a lover of clarity and elegance, one of the greatest *alla prima* painters this country has produced. His contribution was to add new depths of emotion to the twentieth-century vision, to enlarge it with a mysticism more characteristic of the East than the West, and to bring it through exquisite craftsmanship to a highly individual perfection. In the end, having drawn on past and present, he created myths which would live in the future.

Gorky's work sums up a period—a period which developed fauvism, analytic and synthetic cubism, futurism, dadaism, surrealism. He conveys himself in recounting his age. Backed by a peasant tradition which gives his imagination character, he delivers the moods and the passion of a rare and sophisticated personality.

The age he recounts is one Ezra Pound has characterized as that of the "exotic injection." French art received many exotic injections: the Japanese print through Manet, the art of the South Sea Islands through Gauguin, that of the Congo and New Guinea through Picasso. In our own time Lam, Matta and Gorky, themselves born in outlying areas, continued to internationalize Western art.

America has been singularly capable of assimilating foreign ideas and blood and so she has accepted such artists as Gorky, who might more accurately be called an international painter—akin to the writers Gertrude Stein, James Joyce, George Santayana and T. S. Eliot, and the painters Alfred Maurer and Lyonel Feininger, who lived as artists in exile, bringing about by an exchange of impact and receptivity an enriching cross-fertilization of cultures.

Gorky did not use contemporary imagery as did some modern poets —Auden, Spender or C. D. Lewis—that is, locomotives, scientific invention or terminology. He used a contemporary structure, cubism, and a contemporary method, the automatism of surrealism; he also used a contemporary poetic center, the psychology of the unconscious. But for his imagery he drew on his early life or his sensations of nature. If the keys to James Joyce's *Ulysses,* the map and the myth, apply to Dublin and the symbolism of Homer, Gorky's map might be the the fields of Connecticut and Virginia; his myth, the poetry of sex. The artist was as concerned with this vast hidden world seen by the mind alone as with the scarcely more accessible world seen by the eyes. An engineer of the psyche, he crossed from one world into the other, building bridges as he traveled—setting up lines of communication.

I wish to acknowledge here a number of personal debts. I owe much to Mrs. Agnes Phillips but for whose generosity in giving me the right to use freely all letters in the Gorky estate, as well as her personal letters to my husband Wolfgang S. Schwabacher and myself, my book would have been seriously deprived of freshness and authenticity. I wish to thank Gorky's sisters, Mrs. Satenig Avedisian and Mrs. Vartoosh Mooradian, who were kind enough to have their brother's letters translated from the Armenian and painstakingly to search their memories for the biographical facts of Gorky's early life. I am also especially indebted to the late Miss Marny George and Miss Michael West for the gift of their written communications. In the sections dealing with matters of biography in the latter years, the recollections and evaluations of Mrs. Mina

Metzger, Mrs. Margaret La Farge Osborn and Miss Jeanne Reynal, who knew Gorky intimately, have been of great value to me.

To the staff of the Whitney Museum of American Art I owe special thanks. From the beginning of the Gorky project and in all its phases Lloyd Goodrich was my guide and critic. As such, he gave many valuable hours of his time to the drudgery of detailed analysis and constructive criticism, which proved invaluable to me. Beyond this, his vision and recognition of the importance of Gorky's work and of the book heartened and inspired me. I owe him special thanks for his permission to use freely his excellent biographical notes written for the catalogue of the Whitney Museum Memorial exhibition of Gorky's work.

To Meyer Schapiro, who was among the first to recognize Gorky's importance, I am deeply indebted for his perceptive Introduction.

I also wish to record here my deep gratitude to my husband without whose loving faith and encouragement I should never have begun the task. And finally I wish to express my gratitude to Marianne Kris, whose compassionate understanding of the problems involved helped me immeasurably.

Many of Gorky's friends and other individuals in the art world have given me generous assistance. I wish especially to thank the following: Mr. Nathan I. Bijur, Mr. B. Willborg Björck, Mrs. Bruce Bliven, Jr., Mr. Hans Burkhardt, Mr. and Mrs. David Burliuk, Mr. Holger Cahill, Mr. Leo Castelli, Mr. Nicolai Cikovsky, Mr. Bernard Davis, Mr. Stuart Davis, Mr. Wyatt Davis, Mr. and Mrs. Willem de Kooning, Mr. Burgoyne Diller, Mr. Robert Goldwater, Mrs. Edmund Greacen, Mr. Clement Greenberg, Mr. and Mrs. James M. Grossman, Mr. Joseph H. Hirshhorn, Mr. and Mrs. Sidney Janis, Mr. Frederick J. Kiesler, Mr. and Mrs. William Lescaze, Miss Olive M. Lyford, Dr. and Mrs. Warren S. McCulloch, Miss Dorothy C. Miller, Mr. William Miller, Mrs. Edward M. Murphy, Mr. Haic T. Partizian, Mr. and Mrs. Oscar Rosen, Mr. Saul Schary, Mr. Raphael Soyer, Mr. James Johnson Sweeney, Dr. Harry Weiss, Mrs. Joseph D. Weiss and Mr. Erhard Weyhe. Special thanks are due to Mr. Oliver Baker, who did most of the black and white photography, and five of the color photographs.

ETHEL K. SCHWABACHER

My soul listening to the death of
    the twilight.

Kneeling on the far-away soil of
    suffering, my soul is drinking
    the wounds of twilight and of
    the ground; and within, it feels
    the raining dawn of tears.

And all the stars of slaughtered
    lives, so like to eyes grown dim,
    in the pools of my heart this
    evening are dying of despair
    and of waiting.

And the ghost of all the dead to-
    night will wait for the dawn
    with mine eyes and my soul,
    perhaps to satisfy their thirst
    for life, a drop of light will fall
    upon them from on high.

Thirst

ARSHILE GORKY[5]

ARSHILE GORKY

1. Potrait of Vartoosh. 1922.

Oil. 20 x 15. Collection of
Joseph H. Hirshhorn.

Gorky before the Thirties

I Arshile Gorky gave his birthplace variously as Nizhnii-Novgorod, Russia, and Tiflis, Georgia, but he was born, in 1905, at Khorkom Vari, Hayotz Dzore, a small village on Lake Van in Turkish Armenia. When he was four his family moved to Aykestan, a suburb of the city of Van.[6]

Gorky was baptized Vosdanig Adoian. He was the third in a family of four children. There were two older girls: Satenig and Akabe (a stepsister)—and Vartoosh, who, younger by a year than Gorky, was closest to him in childhood and throughout his life. Gorky was very young when his grandparents on both sides died and so had not known them, but at the death of his paternal grandfather was given his name, Manoog, a name he did not like, but by which he is still known to many Armenians. His maternal grandfather, Sarkis der Marderosian, was the last of many generations of priests of the Gregorian Apostolic Church. His father, Sedrag, was a trader who also worked at carpentering to support his large family, including all the paternal aunts and uncles, who lived under his roof as was the Armenian custom. Sedrag Adoian fled, in 1908, from Turkish military service, found his way eventually to America, and was not seen again by his family for many years.

After their father's departure the children were left in the care of their mother Shushanig, a very beautiful woman whose favorite was Gorky. Perhaps the inevitable associations springing from his closeness, as an only son, to a mother who, though not a widow, was without a husband, were felt too deeply by the susceptible boy, and passed into his life as a somewhat overbalanced sense of the unhappiness of things. Possibly a more direct and traumatic effect of the father's departure was Gorky's inability to speak. He did not, indeed, speak until he was five years old, when a tutor his mother had engaged to teach the boy, deciding on a somewhat crude shortcut to his education, took Gorky to a nearby cliff, and by pretending very graphically to jump off effectively shocked him into speaking.

His sisters recall that in the next few years he attended an American mission school and that he took great pride in tending the poplar tree on which his name and birthdate were carved. Accompanied by his sheep dog Zongo, he rode Astighy (his Arabian horse) up into the high Iranian mountains facing Ararat to keep watch with the shepherds; here he took part in their dances and learned the songs which he later sang nostalgically.

On the Island of Akhthamar in Lake Van stands the famous church of Sourp Khatch (Holy Cross).[7] It is distinguished by an extended iconography, sacred and profane—labyrinthine reliefs of myth and folklore replete with the cultural accumulations of underlying Babylonian and Sumerian civilizations, as well as those of Byzantium, Syria and Iran. Doubtless Gorky saw these works, which were enriched with fantastic and delightful forms of hybrid animals and men suggestive of recent surrealism. Perhaps they made what was the non-natural to a Westerner natural to Gorky—the extraordinary, the exaggerated, the fantastic, the mythologic. In any case, we have Gorky's later recollection that the impact of church art on him as a child was powerful.

After the first nine years in Van, Gorky and his family encountered aching misery. During the First World War the Turks had begun a systematic extermination of the Armenians. The Adoians escaped death during the massacres, and fled to Russian Transcaucasia where they settled in Erivan, the present capital of Soviet Armenia. They had lost everything and life was hard. The poverty Gorky experienced in the next years left an ineffaceable memory on the mind of the boy, which he was to express later—obsessively, in paint; and throughout his life he was in terror of encountering it again.

In Erivan Gorky went to an Armenian secondary school, and after school worked at various trades such as typesetting, carpentering, bookbinding and comb-making, but he also drew continually and spent a good part of his earnings for paper, pencils and crayons. For a time the family moved north to Tiflis where Gorky received his first formal education in art, was considered a talented student, and decided to make art his career. However, his mother became ill, and they returned to Erivan in 1918, where, at the age of thirty-eight, she died.

Gorky's two older sisters had gone to America several years earlier, and after his mother's death the boy and his younger sister Vartoosh "Barefooted in rags . . . reached Tiflis with the help of a close Vanetzi friend, Kerza Dikran. In the Georgian capital, another Vanetzi, Mardiros

2. Portrait of Ahko.
c. 1930's.

Oil. 20½ x 15½. Estate of
Arshile Gorky, courtesy
Sidney Janis Gallery.

Sahagian, greatly helped them—giving food and clothing and encouragement to come to America."[8] Joining a party of Armenian emigrants, they
reached New York in 1920 and, after a brief visit in Providence with
Gorky's father,[9] went to live in Watertown, Massachusetts, in the house
of their older sister. "Both began work at the Hood Rubber factory there.
However, Gorky sketched so much on the frames where shoe soles are
placed, that he was fired. . . ."[10] He then visited Providence again for a short

time, attending night classes at the Rhode Island School of Design; here he met Mischa Reznikoff, with whom he was friendly for many years. Reznikoff told me that at this time Gorky studied at the Technical High School which prepared for Brown University's School of Engineering.

When he returned to Boston, about 1923, "The Majestic theater offered him work and he drew pictures of five Presidents on the stage, a minute each."[11] In his spare time he managed to continue with his own painting. According to the recollections of a fellow student at the New School of Design in Boston, Gorky was a student there in 1923 and the following year became an instructor in the life class. She recalls that Gorky was "a tall, serious, young man . . . of great ambition who spent most of his free time in museums and who washed dishes in a restaurant for his meals."[12]

II Gorky rarely dated or signed his works on the face of the canvas in his early period, but preferred to write on the back of the canvas or on the stretcher. As he frequently removed a canvas from the stretcher and reused it without taking the trouble to paint out the old date, this makes the exact placing of these works difficult. He also reworked his canvases at intervals down the years. For instance, *Painting of a Boy* is dated 1924-42. Even though the idea of a painting preceded its realization, sometimes by many years, a canvas finished in 1942 would reflect the style of this period rather than that of the early period in which it was begun. We will therefore place such works in the period of their completion.

In later years he either did not sign his works at all or when he did, at the request of his dealer, it was in a small, fine hand. A lover of anonymity and of the thing in itself, in its condition of absolute beauty, he did not want to distract from the significance of the work. He wanted it to exist in its own right and he wanted the onlooker to remember the painting, not the painter.

Gorky's landscapes and still lifes of the years 1920 to 1925 were dominated by Cézanne. He had probably seen only photographs and reproductions of these works, not the paintings themselves, and so remained unaware of their color. There was something rather heavy-handed in his Cézanne approach, but let us remember that the early works of that master were also gauche and bold. The young Gorky approached the discoveries of the late Cézanne as the young Cézanne approached the works of Manet and Courbet rather crudely, so that these paintings do not look enough like Cézanne to be taken for his work. By the time Gorky came under the influence of Picasso in 1927 he was more able to approximate the paintings of that master.

While Gorky followed the Cézanne influence alone in his landscapes, he turned to Corot, Courbet and Matisse for inspiration in a more personal group of portrait studies and compositions. Even in these early years he injected an autobiographical note into his work, creating the beginnings of a family cycle in a study, *Portrait of Vartoosh* (Fig. 1), dated 1922. Set in an atmosphere of soft, monotone, twilight-drenched gray, the green-ivory of the face, framed by blue-black hair, the quizzically tilted mouth, the somber, fixed eyes of this little portrait bring out her melancholy sensitivity. *Portrait of Ahko* (Fig. 2), begun about the same time, was very probably finished only many years later. Another small painting of 1923, *Portrait of Myself and My Imaginary Wife* (Fig. 3), was the first venture of his free imagination. Thus Gorky has set forth in three independent though parallel directions at once the plastic, or structural, the psychological and the poetically inventive.

Gorky tried all during his life to repudiate the importance of color. Curiously enough, perhaps because this was not a conscious aim, his mastery of the sensuous appeal of color and surface texture was developed early, though in practice he confined himself to certain strongly defined limits. In the paintings described above and in such early works as *Landscape* (1922-23), *Self-Portrait* (1924) and the *Nude* (1926) the color is not

3. Portrait of Myself and My Imaginary Wife. 1923.

Oil. 8½ x 14½. Collection of Joseph H. Hirshhorn.

like stained glass; the colors are not clear, vivid, bright or gay; they are not jewel-like, brilliant. They are tender, powerful, concrete, broad; they absorb rather than reflect; they are like embers rather than flame.

As *Still Life with Skull* (Fig. 4, c. 1925) is apparently so completely imitative of Cézanne, we can here note Gorky's ability to seize the fundamental approach of a master. But inescapably his own personality asserts itself and elements copied at this time eventually became his own, by virtue of being used in a totally different context, purified of the influence that accompanied their development. The heavy drape, painted in tones of sienna brown and deep viridian green with touches of lavender throughout, is considered as a large shape whose outlines are not merely constraining black edges, but rather a series of nuances which take into account the visual sensations arising at all points of the periphery as the tones of the drape meet and affect the tones of the background. Though this painting might seem at first glance to be the work of a student, it is really more than that. It shows Gorky's sensitivity to visual analogies, and is a first intimation of his anthropomorphism of later development.

Gorky could both create pure form out of his own imagination and recognize it whenever it had been created by others. All those who knew him were familiar with his habit of carrying some small book of the masters with him at all times. He would turn the book upside down in order better to enjoy the experience of form detached from content. He analyzed these highly organized shapes, committing them to memory as one might lines of poetry. They excited his imagination, acting as a spur to invention. They also set a qualitative goal. Turning back to the raw material of reality he now saw differently and could not rest until he had translated nature into art.

III At the age of twenty-one Gorky came to New York and soon found a studio on Sullivan Street near Washington Square. In October 1925, he entered the Grand Central School of Art as a student, but shortly became an instructor in the sketch class; the next year he was appointed a full member of the faculty, teaching drawing and painting from then until the end of the 1930-31 term. "The election of Mr. Gorky to the art school faculty," a newspaper reporter, somewhat misled and overbedazzled, wrote, "gives New York . . . a member of one of Russia's greatest artist families, for he is a cousin of the famous writer, Maxim Gorky."[13] At this time Gorky was, it seems, already fervently proselytizing for modern art. He felt that the old masters were bound by convention and rule to painting certain things—"saints, the Madonna, the crucifixion"— and insisted, further, that modern art had gone ahead widely and developed as it never had

4. Still Life with Skull. c. 1925.

   Oil. 33 x 26. Estate of Arshile Gorky, courtesy Sidney Janis Gallery.

a chance to in the hands of the old masters. According to the reporter in the *Post,* Gorky found that there were many good artists in America and is quoted as saying, "Your Twachtman painted a waterfall that was a waterfall in any country, as Whistler's mother was anyone's mother. He caught the universal idea of art. Art is always universal. . . . Art is not in New York, you see; art is in you. Atmosphere is not something New York has, it is also in you."

In 1925, one year after the first surrealist manifesto had been published in Paris by André Breton, New York artists, with few exceptions, were still trying to assimilate the ideas, centering around cubism and futurism, presented so powerfully at the Armory Show of 1913. There were, however, a few Europeans and a very few Americans working in the direction of dada and surrealist ideas in New York, and it is important to note at least certain highlights of their activity, as they were later to have a very strong influence on Gorky. As early as 1912-13 Francis Picabia began to call his "orphic" abstractions by proto-dada names such as *Catch as catch can* and in the June 1913 *Camera Work,* published by Alfred Stieglitz, he announced amorphism, a proto-dada satire on abstract art. In 1915 Alfred Stieglitz published a review, *291,* containing work by Picabia, Picasso, Apollinaire and others. By 1917, Duchamp, who had come to this country two years earlier, published two reviews, *The Blind Man* and *Rongwrong,* and Picabia and Walter Arensberg published a first number of *391;* in 1921 Marcel Duchamp and Man Ray got out one issue of *New York Dada.*

In the next few years there was an increasing flow of dada and surrealist art to this country, and as Gorky was an incessant visitor to galleries he gradually became familiar with the new movements and masters. The two earliest one-man shows of surrealist masters given in this country were de Chirico in 1927 and Miró in 1928, both at the Valentine Gallery. In 1930, Paul Klee was shown at the Museum of Modern Art, and, in the same year the "Painting in Paris" exhibition at the Museum of Modern Art included the fantastic-surrealist group. The most comprehensive show up to that time, the first exclusively surrealist exhibition in America, was held at the Wadsworth Atheneum in Hartford in 1931, and included the work of most of the leading surrealists: Dali, de Chirico, Ernst, Miró, Picasso, Roy, Survage, Masson.[14] Gorky was an inveterate reader of magazines, and loved to prowl for hours at Weyhe's bookstore, where he would quite probably have seen the earliest articles and books on surrealism.

I. The Artist and His Mother. 1926-c. 1936.

Oil. 60 x 50. Whitney Museum of American Art, gift of Julien Levy for Maro and Natasha Gorky in memory of their father.

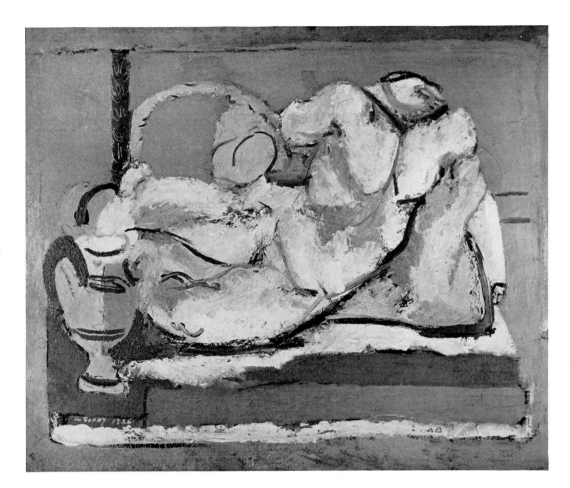

5. The Antique Cast.
1926.

Oil. 36⅛ x 46. Collection
of Mrs. David Metzger.

IV   While Gorky closely followed the general forms of Cézanne he showed
clear signs of power and the beginning of a personal style. In the transitional stage which followed he moved gradually away from Cézanne. As
may be seen in *The Antique Cast* (Fig. 5, 1926), his style remained rep-
resentational, the plastic qualities three-dimensional. But though the
planes are modified by tonal nuances typical of Cézanne, Gorky has given
up that master's fractional approach in favor of the broad unit approach
of Braque and Picasso. Here, as in his later work, we find the marked
opposition of horizontal and vertical—flowing and fixed; the rapid, energetic calligraphy, which runs along crossed diagonals, opposes both the
vertical axis of the vase and the still, flat, monochrome planes that surround it. Drawn from a torso in the Parthenon pediment, this pivotal
painting is pervaded by tragic suggestions, particularly in such passages
as the strange blood-red areas of the diaphragm, reminiscent of Armenian
paintings of Christ nailed to the cross, where blood flows from a reddened
spear wound.

As early as 1926 he began a large portrait of his mother with himself
as a boy (Pl. I), using an old photograph as a model. The two versions

6. Self-Portrait. c. 1937.

Oil. 55½ x 34. Estate of Arshile
Gorky, courtesy Sidney Janis
Gallery.

of this painting, on which he continued to work over a period of ten years, represented his first serious effort to broaden his references. Instead of identifying himself with a single master, he united allusions to the past of Ingres and the present of Picasso and the future of Miró. While holding to the classicism and finish of Ingres, as revivified by Picasso, Gorky did respond to the qualities of floating and suspension in modern painting. Peter Blanc has noted that:

"Today science informs us that we live in a world of shadows so abstract as to make it impossible to form any mental picture of what is really happening. Indeed, as Harvey-Gibson says in *Two Thousand Years of Science*: 'The further science probes into the hidden recesses of the atomic world, the more obscure and shadowy does objective reality seem, the less material and tangible does Nature appear to be.'

"Consequently it seems altogether natural that contemporary painting should depict a shadowy and insubstantial world in which amorphous objects hang suspended in a state of watchful expectation and uncertainty. Miró, Gorky, Baziotes, Stamos, the early Matta, Rothko and others exhibit quite consistently an extreme state of suspension and even in sculpture this quality is evident in such work as Calder's mobiles."[15]

But Gorky did not entirely sacrifice solidity and actuality. Throughout this painting are further evidences of a struggle between two systems of qualities, the transitory and the enduring. The window frame in back of the mother's head floats free of the wall. The windowpane, detached from the frame in which it would normally be held, tilts suspended in space, offering a curious contrast to the statuesque immobility of the two figures, mother and son. The left arm of Arshile is detached, inert. The shoulderless left arm of the mother accentuates the fullness of her body and the weight of her hand, which is treated as an object—circular, enduring, passive. This feeling of arrestedness and permanence contrasts with the delicately adjusted, serpentine flowing of contours and shapes, and the suspended, floating quality of certain areas, such as the mother's apron, which settles with the softness of a cloud or dream upon her solid and formidable body.

The masklike character of the mother's face recalls the succession of great painters from Watteau to Seurat, Lautrec, Rouault and Picasso who were fascinated by clowns and harlequins in whose set, veiled, generalized features they found typified emotions ranging from tragedy to comedy. The mother's eyes under their fine, high brows seem to sink behind their mask and to look into the opaque space of the canvas and backward in time. Through the eyes of the mother we are given, not a view of the world, but a sense of our emotional relationship to it.

35

Because of the pallor of the faces in his portraits Ingres was accused of creating a ghostlike effect (so unlike the ruddy naturalism of his teacher David); Paolo Uccello has been called *"peintre lunaire."* Gorky is a spiritual successor of these two. His work, like the reflection in a mirror, contains all the features of reality but favors essence rather than matter. In the segments of other artists' paintings Gorky has sought the key to their personalities. Out of the segments in which he first betrays his own personality, he seeks to build first a whole picture and then a saga.

About this same time he did a three-quarter-length self-portrait (Fig. 6). This work depends on exquisite adjustments in the free-swinging balance of the floating, nut-brown, putty, olive-green, pale-blue and muted mahogany areas. The effect of the low-keyed palette and the suffusion of light suggesting twilight is abstract, close to the Oriental artist who frequently studied the shadow of bamboo stalks projected on a silk screen by moonlight. Although the body is seen in three-quarter view, which should bring the arm holding the palette nearer the eye of the spectator, Gorky has brought the far arm and hand forward, and thus nearer, giving equal importance to both hands. This equal distribution of attention is characteristic. He no longer upheld the sanctity of the solid object (in this case himself) but emphasized the interplay of background and body areas, and treated the sleeve, the collar, the jacket, and even the arm and hand as pure shape, susceptible of being invaded by space. Once more, as in *The Artist and His Mother,* he has created a curious mixture of potency and impotency—the potency of the inquiring eye and the impotence of the hand which, though it suggests endurance and contained energy, is heavily frozen, immobilized. By what strange alchemy he succeeds in painting himself! The lucid, piercing glance of the deep-set eyes; the long, curving, prominent nose, the sensibility of the mouth, indicating powers of absorption, intuition and effusion, reveal his personality in essence.

During these years Gorky also did many studies of flowers which doubtless enriched his experience and paved the way for the later free use of flower elements. *Three Roses* (Fig. 7) gives off an air of sensuous ease. In the elegant proportions of the white vase we sense Gorky's innate hedonism and essentially aristocratic approach.

It was about this time that he developed certain characteristic technical procedures. He began to build up the paint in thin layers, a method he was to continue with interludes all his life. Advancing from a drawing which he squared off and transferred to the canvas in the academic manner, he varied the tones in each successive layer while maintaining the general over-all balance of color. Traces of the underlying layers, which show as a result of slight recessions in the outlines, reveal these changes

7. Three Roses. c. 1934.

  Oil. 28 x 18. Collection of Mrs. David Metzger.

from green to yellow to red to blue, for example. The result of this clear-cut change in the tones of each reworking is that the final effect is never tired, and the colors are as vital as though they had been done spontaneously. He thought nothing of scraping off the paint from a canvas while it was still wet. "You know," he wrote,[16] "how fussy and particular I am in painting. I am ever removing the paint and repainting the spot until I am completely exhausted." He piled this paint in great mounds, sometimes in tin dishes; and he did the same with paint squeezed fresh from tubes. He would let a skin form on these mounds of paint and loved to pierce them, using the heavy, viscous paint inside, thinned out with a medium which included oil and dammar varnish. This aged paint seemed never to sink in too far but blended with the surface beneath, spreading out heavily like honey.

In 1927, at the age of twenty-three, Gorky entered on a long period of cubist experimentation. At this point a potential colorist, he turned decisively in the direction of form and structure, disciplining his emotions in the rigors of cubist ideology. In a series of still lifes painted from about 1927 to 1932 the forms of fruit, musical instruments, palettes and plaster heads become flattened-out shapes which lie parallel to the surface in traditional cubist style. The object is dissected into its component parts and rearranged according to the dictates of the plastic conception. Calligraphic indications are substituted for literal representation, so that some acknowledgment is made of the spectator's desire for orientation in the real world. The color ranges from dark, warm, earthy tones in the earlier pictures to strong, almost lurid colors in the later ones. The boundaries of the large, powerful shapes are razor-fine. The shapes are not mechanically built up to an outline (Gorky hated the very mention of drawing with a ruler) but in such a way that the swift movement of the brush cuts the adjacent area, giving birth to and defining its shape. This technique follows the practice of Juan Gris, and also suggests the *papier découpé* of the collagists.

The derivative forms of his early cubist works become more personal in the later ones; textures and colors yield to structure; shapes are more dynamic and closely knit into a unified organization of space; areas between shapes take on a life and character of their own. In short, his thought progresses from mere application of the patterns of real objects to concrete representation of the potential object. The potential object is born from the real object and it in turn becomes real.

In *Still Life with Palette* (Fig. 9, 1930), we find interpenetration of shadow and shape, distortion and the arbitrary use of color. We also find a first use of calligraphy in the form to the left of the pitcher spout. The

8. Still Life. 1929.

    Oil. 47 x 60. Estate of Arshile Gorky, courtesy Sidney Janis Gallery.

shadow of the pitcher, used as a shape, is cut across by slats—red and black, brown and blue. This shadow-shape penetrates the white palette, which is tapered into a sharp point beyond the ellipsoidal eye. The bright, strong blue of the over-all background is boldly contrasted with the pink drawer, its circular knob off center, as well as with the red table, the white palette and the black shadows of the objects. Here too the larger space of the canvas is based on a secure horizontal-vertical architecture, while the organization of objects is built up of rhythmically interwoven shapes which activate each other and create a swinging movement as though they were in a slightly swaying hammock.

9. Still Life with Palette. 1930.   Oil. 28 x 36. Collection of Bernard Davis.

The Thirties

I During the early 1930's one-man shows of surrealist leaders were increasingly presented in New York galleries: in 1933 Dali at the Julien Levy, Miró and Masson at the Pierre Matisse; in 1934 Giacometti and Dali at the Julien Levy and Hans Arp at the John Becker Gallery; and in 1935 Miró and Masson at Pierre Matisse, and Dali again at the Julien Levy Gallery. Nineteen thirty-six was the year of the great "International Surrealist Exhibition" at the New Burlington Galleries, London, when 392 items by 58 artists were shown, and Breton, Dali, Eluard and others lectured. That year, too, the Museum of Modern Art in New York gave a large exhibition, "Fantastic Art, Dada, Surrealism," with a catalogue edited by Alfred Barr, containing an introduction by him and essays by Georges Hugnet. Gorky was not then known as a surrealist and was not included in the exhibition, although some Americans were—for example, Blume, Calder, Cornell and Man Ray. Few painters as yet fully understood surrealism; as Julien Levy pointed out in the first book exclusively on surrealism to be published in this country:

". . . Joseph Cornell must be mentioned as one of the very few Americans at the present time who fully and creatively understands the surrealist viewpoint. Generally speaking, with the exception of Man Ray who is a veteran surrealist, there is in America considerable misunderstanding of the surrealist point of view, and the numerous semi-surrealist efforts of the past few years have only elaborated superficial details and idiosyncrasies without ever reaching below the surface to a more complete contact with surrealism as a *point of view*."[17]

In enumerating the various opportunities for seeing and reading about surrealist art presented during these years I do not wish to tire the reader, but rather to point out how the growing number of exhibitions and articles affected Gorky and how the climate of the New York art world was gradually changing from the cooler, more temperate one of cubism to the more variable and even violent one of surrealism. If cultivation had the advantage of harmony, perfection and radiance, wilderness had the advantage of profusion: unordered, tumbled, thickly intertwined, unknown, unexpected. Gorky knew that both tendencies existed within himself and set himself to battle and experiment with the full range of possibilities.

II Gorky had early established some reputation for himself in the art world. The first dealer to handle Gorky's work after he came to New York was J. B. Neumann. His first showing in a museum was at the newly founded Museum of Modern Art in 1930, in the exhibition "46 Painters and Sculptors under 35." He was also shown by the Société Anonyme in 1931. In 1932 he was sufficiently well known to be invited to become a charter member of the "Abstraction, Création, Art Non-figuratif" group which was formed in Paris and included Albers, Calder, Dreier, Hélion, Holty, Moholy-Nagy and Seligmann.

His first one-man exhibition of thirty-seven paintings done from 1926 to 1930 was in February 1934, at the Mellon Galleries, Philadelphia, managed by Philip Boyer. The critical response was excellent; Holger Cahill, the first well-known American critic to show enthusiasm for Gorky's work, noted that he had "an extraordinary inventiveness and fertility in creating special arrangements both precise and harmonious," and that he contributed to contemporary American expression "a note of intellectual fantasy which is very rare in the plastic art of this country."[18] The architect F. J. Kiesler also befriended him and perceptively caught something of the spirit of the man and his work, characterizing him as the ". . . spirit of Europe in the body of the Caucasus, getting the feel of American soil," and noted that in Gorky, "Unswerving, critical reason seeks the quintessence of Picasso-Miró drunkenly to absorb them, only to exude them again in deep slumber. . . . This Caucasian stranger," he further prophesied, "having just quenched his hunger and thirst, is ready to shoulder down the doors into a land of his own. . . ."[19] Stuart Davis also made a statement pointing out that Gorky was a painter who had "proved his intelligence in painting by the progressive elimination of formulas which have alternated in the education and dissolution of the people who are interested in the arts," and added that, "In place of these formulas he tentatively substitutes several structures which have equal validity and much greater topical value and do not involve promises."[20] Indeed, Gorky was not again to have critical support of this caliber and quality for many years, though one-man exhibitions of his drawings were held at the Boyer Gallery, Philadelphia, in September 1935, and at the Guild Art Gallery, New York, that December; and paintings at the Boyer Gallery in New York three years later. Further, he was shown consistently at the Whitney Museum, beginning with the important exhibition "Abstract Painting in America," in February 1935, when four of his paintings were included and one reproduced in the catalogue (along with Marin, Stella and Weber) and from 1936 on, in all but four of its annual painting exhibitions and in four drawing annuals. These one-man and group exhibitions, however, did little to improve Gorky's finances.

III Among Gorky's early friends was Stuart Davis, ten years his senior, already in command of his own idiom, and, of course, comparatively well established in the art world. In an article, written after Gorky's death, he recalls, "I remember knowing Arshile Gorky in 1929 after I came back from Europe, but have no recollection before that. I may have met him in Romany Marie's[21] through Paul Gaulois or John Graham. In any case we became close friends and saw each other often."[22] At this time Gorky was living "in a fairly decent artistic-type studio on the edge of the slums near Washington Square on Sullivan Street," and had equipped it with "the paraphernalia popularly believed to be the appropriate sign of the true artist." Stuart Davis was flabbergasted by the quantities of material Gorky had acquired: "Outside of an art store I had never seen anything like this col-

10. Objects. 1932.

Ink. 22¼ x 30. Museum of Modern Art, Van Gogh Purchase Fund.

lection of properties in one place before—nor since, for that matter. The question of how he acquired this truly impressive stockpile and kept it replenished was raised from time to time, but no really clear picture of the feat was ever arrived at." Davis was duly impressed by the "dramatic impact" of this man whom "Nature had provided . . . with a tall, dark and impressive aspect" which he brought "to its maximum intensity by the adoption of a black velour hat pulled low over the eyes, and a black overcoat buttoned tight under the chin and extending to the ankles." Davis further recalls that Gorky "was intensely interested in ideas and talked enthusiastically

11. Drawing. 1929-32.

Ink. 21⅝ x 27¼. Estate of Arshile Gorky, courtesy Sidney Janis Gallery.

about them," and that "He recited tales of his various exploits with florid embellishments and boastings that held the attention of his listeners, because a good deal of the objectivity of humor was included . . . . The studio, the costume and the talk added up to a dramatization of his natural gifts which made him an unforgettable personality." By 1931 their friendship was on such a sound footing that Stuart Davis asked Gorky to write a critical appraisal for a feature article on his work, to appear in the magazine *Creative Art*—"I chose Gorky, which indicated how sure I was of his friendship and sincere liking for my work." Though Gorky was a younger man Stuart Davis admired his work and recalls that when necessary he defended it:

44

"During the period that I knew him, Gorky's work was strongly influenced by certain styles of Picasso. This was apparent to everybody, and there was a tendency to criticize him as a naive imitator. I took a different view and defended his work at all times. . . . It must be remembered that at that remote period the exponents of modern art were much less numerous than they are today, and they needed to maintain a solid front against the Squares of every ilk who were always out to subvert it. The same thing goes on today because the Squares are always with us, but the ratio of strengths has changed. Under those conditions I would automatically have supported Gorky's work and kept questions of disagreement inside the family circle. But I had no equivocal opinions about it. I took it for what it was—the work of a talented artist in the process of development, and one who had the intelligence and energy to orient himself in the direction of the most dynamic ideas of the time."

While the generous and perspicacious article Gorky wrote about his friend Stuart Davis for *Creative Art* showed his recognition of the importance of Davis's work as a leading American painter, it also defined his own position in regard to cubism. As there are so few written records of Gorky's ideas on art I will quote it at length.

". . . Yet the silent consequences of Stuart Davis move us to the cool and intellectual world where all human emotions are disciplined upon rectangular proportions. Here these relations take us to the scientific world where all dreams evaporate and logic plays its greatest victory, where the physical world triumphs over all tortures, where all the clumsiness dies, and leaves only the elements of virtue, where the esthetic world takes new impulse for new consequences. Oh, what a glorious prospect! This man, this American, this pioneer, this modest painter, who never disarranges his age, who works to perfect his motives, who renders clear, more definite, more and more decided new forms and new objects. He chooses new rules to discipline his emotions. He gives new shape to his experiences with new sequences—orange, red, yellow, green, brown and chalk-like white, metallic grays and dull blacks, profound spaces with sky-like blues stabilized upon rectangular directions. He takes a new position upon the visible world. This artist, whether he paints eggbeaters, streets or pure geometrical organizations, expresses his constructive attitude toward his successive experiences. He gives us symbols of tangible spaces, with gravity and physical law. He, above his contemporaries, rises high—mountain-like! Oh, what clarity! One he is, and one of but few, who realizes his canvas as a rectangular shape with two dimensional surface plane. Therefore he forbids himself to poke humps and holes upon that potential surface. This man, Stuart Davis, works upon that platform where are working the giant painters of the century—Picasso, Léger, Kandinsky, Juan Gris—bringing to us new utility, new aspects, as does the art of Uccello. They take us to the supernatural world behind reality where once the great centuries danced.

45

12. Drawing. 1929-32.

Ink. 22 x 30. Estate of Arshile Gorky, courtesy Sidney Janis Gallery.

"Yet there are numbers of critics, artists, and public suspended like vultures, waiting in the air for the death of the distinctive art of this century, the art of Léger, Picasso, Miró, Kandinsky, Stuart Davis. They forget that while the artist never works outside his time, yet his art will go on to be merged gradually into the new art of a new age. There will be no short stop. We shall not, contrary to the expectation of these people, hear of the sudden death of cubism, abstraction, so-called modern art. These critics, these artists, these spectators who wait for a sudden fall are doomed to disappointment. They have merely not understood the spiritual movement and the law of direct energy of the centuries, and they can never have understood the spiritual meaning of any form of art. If they could but realize that energy is a spiritual movement, and that they must conceive of working under a law of universal esthetic progress, as we do in science, in mathematics, in physics.

"The twentieth century—what intensity, what activity, what restless, nervous energy! Has there in six centuries been better art than cubism? No. Centuries will go past—artists of gigantic stature will draw positive elements from cubism.

"Clumsy painters take a measurable space, a clear definite shape, a rectangle, a vertical or horizontal direction, and they call it blank canvas, while every time one stretches canvas he is drawing a new space. How could they ever have understood cubism or the art of the twentieth century? How could they even conceive of the elements that go into the making of art? How could they accept tranquility and expansion as elements of feeling in painting? . . .

"Because Stuart Davis realizes the invisible relations and phenomena of this modern time, he is the visible point to the progressive mind in his country."[23]

But by 1934 their friendship came to an end. As Stuart Davis put it: "In the early part of 1934 the economic situation for artists became so bad that they were forced to look around for ways and means to save themselves. They were shoved together by mutual distress, and artist organizations of one kind or another began to form as a natural result. I was in these things from the beginning and so was Gorky. I took the business as seriously as the serious situation demanded and devoted much time to the organizational work. Gorky was less intense about it and still wanted to play. In the nature of the situation, our interests began to diverge and finally ceased to coincide altogether. Our friendship terminated and was never resumed."

This, of course, is Stuart Davis's account of the situation. It seems very doubtful, however, that Gorky's attitude was "playful." More probably his point of view was simply different and, characteristically, firmly held. In these five years of friendship Gorky's growth from so rapt an admiration for the older artist into fuller maturity and independence may have resulted in the inevitable clash of two strong personalities and the end of a friendship.

13. Drawing. 1929-32.

Ink. 14 x 17. Estate of Arshile Gorky, courtesy Sidney Janis Gallery.

In 1930 Gorky moved to 36 Union Square, two blocks from the Eighteenth Street Lexington subway station. Four flights of dark, dusty stairs, a dirty green door hand-painted in small but conspicuous yellow letters, "A. Gorky," and a long foyer led to the high-ceilinged, enormous studio; two smaller rooms, used as sleeping quarters, and a kitchenette led off beyond.

Gorky did not follow the so-called bohemian tradition; he was punctual and orderly. He kept his studio scrupulously clean, scrubbing the floor weekly so that it finally had the bleached tone of driftwood; the large palette on the table, under the frosted slanting window, was left in just the state of low-lustered sheen he liked best. There was nothing haphazard about the piles of leftover or unused paint; there was no bit of material that he was indifferent to; the brushes, of which he had great quantities, bristle, camel's hair, of various sizes, round, flat, worn or new, were washed with soap and water after work; there were bottles of ink, pens, quill pens, crayons in profusion; a Greek head and hand, a porcelain fruit dish, a vase or so stood or lay about; also a few art books, an old small phonograph and a half-dozen records of Russian songs. And on the wall, where he would certainly have liked to hang the paintings of his choice, were the nearest substitute he could afford—life-size photographs of the works of Ucello and Ingres.

The great excitement of 36 Union Square lay in the feeling it evoked of work done there, work in progress, day and night, through long years of passionate, disciplined and dedicated effort. Gorky took pride in the massive pile of his work. Some two hundred of his paintings were carefully stacked, stretcher against stretcher, in a separate room off the foyer used only for storage. He knew where each painting was and could find any given one when he wanted to revise it, as he so often did; or to use some detail in a new effort to solve some problem, whether of this year or fifteen years earlier, that in the actual moment was absorbing his attention.

Willem de Kooning has described his response to Gorky and 36 Union Square in the following letter published in *Art News,* January 1949:

"In a piece on Arshile Gorky's memorial show—and it was a very little piece indeed—it was mentioned that I was one of his influences. Now that is plain silly. When, about fifteen years ago, I walked into Arshile's studio for the first time, the atmosphere was so beautiful that I got a little dizzy and when I came to, I was bright enough to take the hint immediately. If the book-keepers think it necessary continuously to make sure of where things and people come from, well then, I come from 36 Union Square. It is incredible to me that other people live there now. I am glad that it is about impossible to get away from his powerful influence. As long as I keep it with myself I'll be doing all right. Sweet Arshile, bless your dear heart."

OPPOSITE:

II. Waterfall. c. 1943.

Oil. 60½ x 44½.
Estate of Arshile Gorky,
courtesy Sidney Janis
Gallery.

V Around the corner from 36 Union Square, at Fourth Avenue and Nineteenth Street, was a coffee shop; Gorky took coffee at all times of the day and night from a counter and with doughnuts when he was hungry. Across from the shop, on Union Square, speakers usually harangued a sparse, sprawling crowd. Zigzag from here was Fourteenth Street, tawdry by day and neon-lighted by night. Beyond Fourteenth Street was Fifth Avenue and then Washington Square and Greenwich Village.

After work and between cups of coffee he would often walk in this direction, into and past the uncanny profundities of the red, no-red, and emerald green, no-green, stop-go lights. He would sometimes continue to Washington Square, where, when the outdoor art show was in progress, painters hung their works against the walls of their individual stalls. Some sat doing portrait sketches, others just waited for spectators and buyers. Gorky loved the work of these simple men. He bent over this work and that, saying, "Beautiful." He had an unfoolable eye. Picking his way here and there he discovered the original, the formulated, the good work, congratulated the artist, and went on. So much talent existed modestly waiting its day.

Returning home he entered the dark hallway, mounted the shabby uneven steps, floor after floor, until he reached his door. Then, as usual, he

14. Image in Xhorkom.
c. 1932.

Pencil. 18⅝ x 24½. Estate of Arshile Gorky, courtesy Sidney Janis Gallery.

49

stood looking at his painting across the foyer and across the room. He always liked to study the great, general plan of the painting and to ask himself, did it hold from a distance? Was it inevitable, steady, self-contained, like outward reality? Was it rooted in its own soil, growing toward its own sky? After a long while he moved forward to inspect it from closer up. Then he looked swiftly to the side for a moment where the large Ingres self-portrait hung before he leaned forward to look closely at his own work.

We may follow him as he looked around the studio once more, his attention caught by the Uccello— What was its secret? Certainly it was to the far past of art his heart now turned, as to the far past of his life, the irretrievably gone—yet beloved. In art he wished, however, to find the past not only immortalized and placed in museums to be worshipped, but reincarnated in the present. And still he was not satisfied; he longed to create in the immediacy of feeling which opened up within him, as images poured through his brain.

Gorky would have stood, looking at the painting. Nervous but not restless, he had the isolation and stance of a mountain man accustomed to long watches. His attention was never removed from seeing. Finally he started to paint, mixing tones on a very large palette. At the foot of the easel was a paper flower to which he referred, working against this hard and inescapable token of reality.

VI The depression which began in 1929 so impoverished Gorky that he was unable to buy paints and canvas. Through 1932, he was forced for a long time to work chiefly on a series of drawings (Figs. 10-14). Most of these drawings, done in pen and ink, or occasionally in pencil, were studies related to a projected panel which he later executed in oils. This panel was a horizontal series of independent compositions divided by vertical elements, including a column directly in the center—a conception inspired by Paolo Uccello's connected composition, *The Miracle of the Host*. Analysis of Uccello and Piero della Francesca had convinced Gorky that the use of such independent but related compositions was a powerful design. But the objects he placed in these areas were completely modern, personalized, plastic creations in which he cultivated the effect of dislocation, which was one of the cardinal theories of surrealism. To quote André Breton:

"Super-reality must in any case be a function of our will to put everything out of place (and of course (a) one may go so far as to put a hand out of place by isolating it from an arm; (b) the hand gains thereby *qua* hand, and (c) in speaking of putting out of place we are not referring merely to the possibility of action in space.)"[24]

15. Nighttime, Enigma and Nostalgia. 1929-34.
    Oil. 36 x 48. Martha Jackson Gallery.

Surrealist in feeling, the shapes Gorky used suggest the marvelous or magical, dream-world images and moods. Whether consciously or unconsciously conceived, the imagery of the arrow, the staircase, the palette, the column, the sphere, the antique head abstracted into a phallic shape, the breastlike pyramids, the bird form, the seed, cover a wide range of erotic symbols. Gorky first set forth here the themes of fertilization and of the labyrinth which continued to obsess him throughout his life. In these drawings he has created forms stripped completely of the seduction of outward appearance. Used as plastic ideograms, they create a mysterious, analogical world, drenched in moonlit blackness. Now he achieves, at last, exact images of hallucinatory visions, whose beginnings may have gone back to his childhood.

A portion of the right-hand composition, developed independently, exists in some thirty variations. To build up form he used a variety of pen strokes, piling layer upon layer, freely, in the rhythm of the natural arm swing; at other times there are firm crosshatchings in which the line varies in weight. These varieties of texture gave a wide range of color and vibration. At times he washed off or erased surfaces before building them up again. This resulted in an aging of the paper itself; it looked like the paper of an old-master drawing. The superimposed material, ink in this case, became amalgamated with the original material, the paper, to form a different substance. Scorning newness, Gorky achieved a surface that suggests the erosion of mountains, the slow filtering down of layers of soil on the earth. In this patient way nature creates a new topography. Gorky imitated nature's processes, subordinating the will to make to the deeper will to arrive at a creation.

The same portion of this set of drawings is also developed in an oil study, 1929-34 (Fig. 15). While light flows around the objects, as in the drawing (where it is black!) he has not yet learned how to make it penetrate them. Instead of taking on an aerated, scintillating, phosphorescent dream texture, the shapes in the painting are solid, real. The surrealist mood persists, however, in the profound state of mind he induces by the tension of shifting emphasis between poles of black and white, the two colors most expressive of the eternal constants—life and death—and in the immobile desolation of the gray.

VII Although a few paintings of the early 1930's anticipated his later surrealist tendencies, instead of going further in this direction, in the years 1933 to 1936 Gorky entered a new period of formal discipline. He painted several large canvases, almost purely abstract, predominantly geometrical in form, and frequently based on a white background. Closely related to Pi-

16. Composition with Head. c. 1935.

Oil. 78 x 62. Estate of Arshile Gorky, courtesy Sidney Janis Gallery.

53

casso's white paintings of 1927 and 1928, they grew out of studio interiors with large wall spaces containing still-life objects, flattened out in the typical cubist manner (*e.g.*, Figs. 16, 17). In these paintings Gorky piled layer upon layer of heavy paint until he sometimes built the surface an inch above the canvas; and by an extravagance calculated in its seeming excess reached the essential in a new way. He had always admired the raised surfaces of Cézanne, obtained in patient search for the exact fullness of form; but while Cézanne's surfaces resemble fine porcelain, Gorky's suggest the low reliefs on the spacious walls of Armenian buildings. At times the shapes and spaces are so rigorous and clean as to suggest the purism of Mondrian and the geometric constructivism of Malevich. But Gorky evidently learned from this type of experience that geometric purism had little to offer him, and abandoned any further attempts in this direction.

17. Organization. 1933-36.

Oil. 49¾ x 60. Estate of Arshile Gorky, courtesy Sidney Janis Gallery.

18. Image in Xhorkom.
c. 1936.

Oil. 32⅞ x 43. Collection of
Miss Jeanne Reynal.

Renewed by this immersion in the work of Picasso, Gorky was now ready for more independent creation. About 1936 he embarked on a new phase in which the geometric forms of the preceding years were transformed into freer organic forms, strongly rhythmical, and in which there was a growing element of fantasy and symbolism. Among the most powerful of these works are the four versions of *Image in Xhorkom*. The essential idea of this series had been developed in a drawing of about 1932 (Fig. 14). Gorky now gave it full substance, emphasizing different plastic and poetic aspects in each version. In the *Image in Xhorkom* (Fig. 18) one observes something incommensurable, a certain deceptive distinctness, and at the same time a mysterious depth. The heavy gray of the background yields up forms which are a transformation of reality. Even the clearest figure has a comet's tail attached to it, suggesting the uncertain, the nebulous; a similar twilight shrouds the structure.

Though the emotional impact of *Image in Xhorkom* (Fig. 18) is forceful, the largest of the four versions (Fig. 19) is a more advanced plastic expression; the planes are established with greater clarity and the images have crystallized. The background plane moves forward and the frontal plane moves into the depth, so that the interlocking of shapes and spaces occurs no longer as in a bas-relief, but in an extended surface, elaborated contrapuntally. In the smaller painting the shape of the woman evokes an idol; in the larger, this shape, metamorphosed into an albatross, takes on the aspect of a magical emblem.

Though Gorky continued to advance in the direction of surrealism, works such as the Whitney Museum's *Painting* (Fig. 20) were still close to Picasso. The bird image, developed in the ink drawings of about 1932, emerges here in paint, singular, savage and somehow suggestive of a harshly primitive stolidity. The curious staring bird eye, which holds one immobilized in silent expectancy, has the mesmerizing power of animal innocence, like the unbending eye of a child. This round eye shape reappears no less hauntingly as the "eye" of the palette, as the "knot" of the tassel, as the "eye" of the leaf, strangely transformed into a bird head. In its formal function it may be considered as a hub around which the forms pivot stiffly, like mechanical dolls.

In *Enigmatic Combat* (Fig. 21, c. 1936) Gorky brought the Picasso influence to its furthest usefulness. After painting this sumptuous work he finally abandoned the use of heavy black outlines, prismatic structure, the definitely determined background and foreground plane and closed spaces. This painting marks the triumphant climax of a long apprenticeship. The saturated, intense, powerfully orchestrated colors increase the dynamics of this tightly integrated composition. The black line, doubled during part of its extent by a white one which highlights it and establishes new rhythms, adding variety to what might have been an overdetermined stiffness in the plan, is so heavy that it suggests the lead binding used in stained glass windows, giving a Byzantine dimension to this modern style.

We have spoken of the fact that Gorky frequently looked at nature through the eyes of some master, and at the work of one master through the eyes of another. He had seen Ingres and Cézanne through the eyes of Picasso, then Picasso and Klee through the eyes of Miró. Still later he was to see Duchamp through the eyes of Matta. This did not diminish his own highly original way of seeing; nothing could. In fact this was a genuine part of that very way. He used their eyes as well as his own, impersonally, as purveyors of fact or artifact. What he saw became letters of an alphabet; using that alphabet he composed words, sentences, poems.

The influence of Miró on Gorky grew out of a natural affinity for his way of seeing, which approached Eastern art more closely than Western.

19. Image in Xhorkom. 1936.

Oil. 36 x 48. Estate of Arshile Gorky, courtesy Sidney Janis Gallery.

20. Painting. 1936-37.
  Oil. 38 x 48. Whitney Museum of American Art.

As early as 1928 he had seen the work of Miró at the Valentine Gallery. By 1936 Gorky had adopted Miró's use of a continuous background, but with a difference. Anyone who has gazed up into the sky directly at the sun will probably have experienced the optical illusion that the sun is a hollow cut out of a blue expanse. In the late 1930's Gorky's shapes give this impression. They indicate the area of an object but not its rounded form. Where Miró's objects seem to float in front of a backdrop, Gorky's appear to be cut out of it. In his murals Gorky had used collage. Now, instead of pasting, which was a way of building area upon area, he cut out the shapes from the larger area. He relied on the use of flat and concave and almost entirely abandoned the use of the convex or rounded. By deliberately leaving his space uncluttered, by leading his lines off the canvas, as nearly as possible ignoring the limiting effect of its physical edge, Gorky excited an awareness of open space; his energy filled the canvas, overflowed it, suggested further horizons.

VIII In 1935 Gorky met Marny George, a Middle Western girl ten years younger than himself, who had come to New York to learn something about fashion art. As she recollected many years later, he wooed her with poetry. "I am a poet," he would say often, and one day a lovely gardenia tree accompanied a poem. After a short courtship he married her—but, unfortunately, their brief marriage was to be a continual battle. "It seems," Marny George wrote,[25] "the very moment we were married the battle began. . . . 'Ferocious as a giant, tender as a little child' he used to say of himself. How very true! Arshile tried to break the barriers [between them], first with tenderness, then with force. But the barriers grew in direct relation to the violence. It was a tragedy for us both."

Their marriage was further complicated by poverty. Though Gorky had a capacity for enjoying life, its work, its gifts, there was always an undercurrent of nervous distress. He could never escape (nor had life helped him in this respect) from the haunting anxiety implanted in him in early childhood. Then he had experienced the horrors of the Turkish invasion, followed by famine and poverty. But there was beauty too, the eagerness and ecstasy of the awakening boy; thus fear and beauty were early brought into close, perhaps inseparable, association in his mind, and throughout his life there was, beyond the real need, an obsessive need to keep poverty at bay.

His friends had again and again noted Gorky's poverty. Marny George sympathetically: "We had very little money. . . . But in spite of usually having to scrape for food (which Arshile often cooked in or over a wood . . . stove) he could never pass by an art supply store without emptying

21. Enigmatic Combat.
c. 1936.

Oil. 35¾ x 48. San Francisco Museum of Art, gift of Jeanne Reynal.

his pockets and coming home with new tubes of paint and brushes." This was an understatement, as Gorky frequently ran into debt—at one time he owed as much as $600 to his art-supplies dealer—and Marny George recalls the precautions he took to protect himself from the demands of dealer and landlord. "At this time our studio was being repainted by the landlord. (The studio was always being repainted.) There was an entrance hall, shut off by a door from the main studio, and with no windows. This Arshile painted black so when someone knocked on the door he could open it and peek through the crack and so see who it was without being seen. He refused to have a telephone and people would usually have to send telegrams or tuck notes under the door to contact him." And again his friend and pupil, the painter Hans Burkhardt: "Times were very hard for Gorky, and most of the time he was without funds, living mainly on coffee and doughnuts. Whenever I came to the studio, I would bring him

60

food, and sometimes I would ask him to have dinner with me at some nearby restaurant. But his pride would not permit him really to satisfy his hunger at these times. Numerous times he begged me to buy one of his paintings, so that he might be able to pay his rent, and not be evicted from his studio."[26] And once again Stuart Davis, though in this case half-derisively, as though poverty were a pose: "He had a continuous complaint about poverty, which was real enough, and sought to liquidate any vestige of doubt in an already long-convinced audience by displaying holes, patches and rags in the garments which he wore under the overcoat."[27]

Gorky's first marriage, to Marny George, had the quality of a passing love affair. As a foreigner he had had no frame of reference by which to assess the character of an American girl. He had fallen in love with beauty, and Marny George was beautiful: with love itself, perhaps, as he imagined it. He had felt he could create a woman, as he had created his art. "Arshile wanted," Marny George wrote, "to form and mold me into the woman he wanted for his wife." He instinctively had tried to use the same process he had used in his work, a process of trial and error, infinitely patient renewed efforts toward the full-fleshed embodiment of an ideal perfection whose shadow lay cool, abstract and substanceless on the interior wall of his mind.

His attempt to create a wife was doomed to failure. Human material was not as malleable as paint. "One day," as Marny George put it, "he reached the end of his endurance. He hauled out my suitcase and threw my few belongings into it, carried it down the dark, rickety stairs leading from the studio, set it on the sidewalk and went back—to God knows what."

IX   One year later Gorky became infatuated with the painter Michael West. He sent her love letters written in a curious mixture of his own words—very simple, human and intimate—and excerpts from French poetry: "Lady Love" by Paul Eluard,[28] and portions of a prose poem entitled, "Simulation of General Paralysis Essayed" by André Breton in collaboration with Paul Eluard;[29] the letters were particularly untrammeled in expression and contained linguistic adornments which quite possibly suggested to Gorky the Persian and Armenian courtship songs of his people (in any case he used them in this way) and religious imagery—here Gorky, not entirely at home in a foreign language, probably missed the fact that the religious phrases were rather garbled, and gathered from them only a sense of the familiar litanies of his childhood. Perhaps, too, his use of these poems in a love letter indicated his difficulty in finding a compromise or balance between the love–culture of his people, exotic from our point of view, and that of his own environment. But in spite of repressive forces and language difficulties he now poured out a report of his doings, his longings and his love in three letters, which follow unabridged. The first was written after visiting Michael West in Rochester:

"11 August/36

"My precious Love

"Now that I have got over all the fatigues of the journey, two real impressions remain with me, In the first place, the sweet sensation of perfect and profound love which unites us one to another, and next, the pleasantness of you my Carinne and your work.

"I miss you terribly and this place seems to me so big and unhappy because you are not with me.

"My little darling you are in a very charming place all the lovely country not to grand, but very intimate, very human and rather celtic with gaiety of its own, has made a great impression on me.

"My heart bleeds on thy mouth and closes on thy mouth on all red chestnut-trees of the avenue of thy mouth where we are on our way through thy shining dust to lie us down amidst the meteors of the beauty that I adore my great one who art so beautiful that I am happy to adorn my treasures with thy presence with thy thought and with thy name that multiplies the facets of the ecstasy of my treasures with thy name that I adore because it wakes an echo in all the mirrors of beauty of my splendour my original woman my scaffolding of rose-wood thou are the fault of my fault of my very great fault as Jesus Christ is the woman of my cross—twelve times twelve thousand one hundred and forty-nine times I have loved thee with passion on the way and I am crucified to north east west and north for thy kiss of radium and I want thee and in my mirror of pearls thou are the breath of him who shall not rise again to the surface and who loves thee in adoration my woman lying upright when thou art seated combing thyself.

"I love you so much my little Carinne and I kiss you passionately from the head to the foot of your lovely body and pray the warm sun for your happiness and the success of your work, I love you tenderly, and wait feverishly for the first chance of seeing you again of possessing you fully and fondly.

"In flames.

Arshile"

The second was written from Long Island:

[*Undated*]

"My precious love

"Thou my great one whom I adore beautiful as the whole earth and in the most beautiful stars of the earth that I adore thou my great woman adored by all the powers of the stars beautiful with the beauty of the thousands of millions of queens who adorn the earth the adoration that I have for thy beauty brings me to my knees to beg thee to think of me I am brought to my knees I adore thy beauty think of me thou my adorable beauty my great beauty whom I adore I roll the diamonds in the moss loftier than the forest whose most lofty hair of thine think of me—forget me not my little woman when possible at Ingle-nook on the sand of emerald—look at thyself in my hand that keeps me steadfast on the whole world so that thou mayest recognize me for what I am my dark-fair woman my beautiful one my foolish one think of me in paradises my head in my hands.

 "Carinne my love I miss you terribly. I am sending you the picture hope you like it

Arshile"

22. Battle at Sunset with the God of the Maize. 1936.

Oil. 8 x 10. Collection of Joseph H. Hirshhorn.

And the third, on his return from a visit to his sister Vartoosh:

"Aug 24—1936
New York City

"My very Dear Love

 "Carinne I kiss you with all my heart, press you and hug you Dear Love —to the silence of her who leaves my dreams.

    "She is standing on my lids
  And her hair is in my hair
  She has the colour of my eye
  She has the body of my hand
  In my shade she is engulfed
  As a stone against the sky

She will never close her eyes
And she does not let me sleep
And her dreams in the bright day
Make the suns evaporate
And me laugh cry and laugh
Speak when I have nothing to say.

"INFORMATION: Have received your sweet letter long ago— I am so glad that you are working with Faith portrait. Please write to me more about. Beloved, I am very tired; I have done nothing but rush from one place to another, with my murals and started a painting 14 x 9 ft this morning have been to Boston with Vartoosh my sister and last week end to country."

"Recognize me for what I am. Think of me in paradises my head in my hands," Gorky had written; but Michael West, though not unwilling to try, had been unable to do this. Their long and passionate sessions together ended, as she later expressed it,[30] "in complete frustration"; while "leaving his presence was agony," separation was the inevitable outcome of a relationship which was, at bottom, to use her words, "a platonic love of two artists driven by love for work . . . obsessed with painting to a fanatical point"—to a point which, perhaps, precluded love; thus, it seems, infatuation did not steady into love but guttered down, and Gorky was once more alone with his dreams and his phantom companions.

X   From 1936 to 1942 a series of paintings continues Gorky's personal saga. Joined to a growing element of intellectual fantasy there is a delightful storytelling faculty. The heart of his imagination had been nourished on folklore and folk song of a robust peasant character; so, in the father-to-son peasant tradition, Gorky transmitted some of the tales which had doubtless held his forefathers' interest during the long winter nights in the mountains of Tiflis. The fluency of these paintings, so entirely Gorky in the personal quality of the synthesis, and conveying the song of his people with singular purity and charm, should interest those critics of Gorky's work who believed that he only became himself in the last two or three years of his life.

In several paintings of the middle 1930's, though the imagery was only lightly indicated, one might sense a battlefield in which the form and force of a warrior drawn up short in full gallop, in the act of throwing his spear, was caught by the camera eye of the artist; quite possibly memories of saints on horseback, in the act of lancing a dragon or other animal, such as those that cover a large part of the Church of Akhthamar, had fused with memories of similar representations in *La Chasse* by Paolo

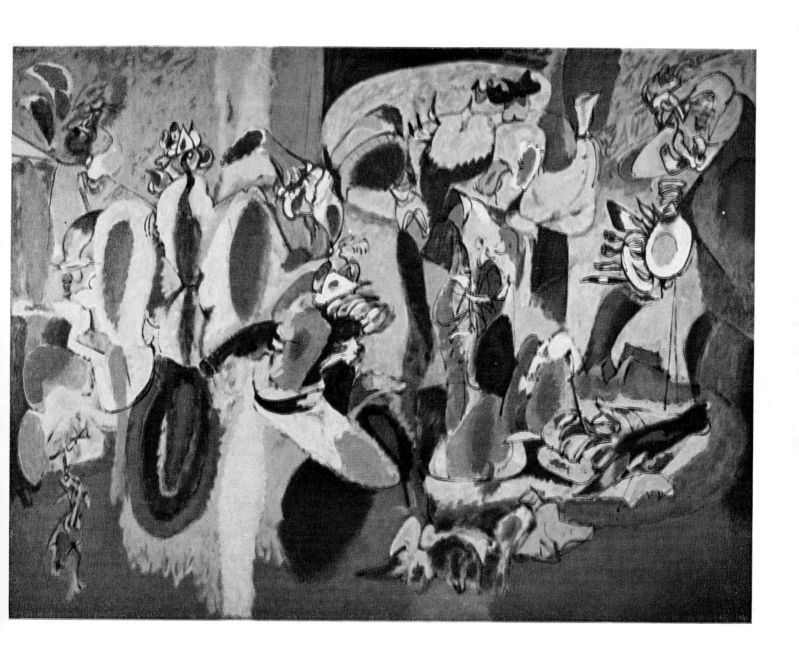

III. The Liver is the Cock's Comb. 1944.

Oil. 73 x 98. Albright Art Gallery, Buffalo.

23. Child of an Idumean Night. 1936.

Oil. 8¾ x 12. Collection of Joseph H. Hirshhorn.

Uccello, with the result that now, thoroughly ripened in the depths of memory, varied images of horse and rider could emerge, as if spontaneously, in full flower.

The eight versions of the *Garden in Sochi* (Figs. 26-29) painted from 1938 to 1942 are brilliant variations on a theme whose source was the memory of a garden familiar to his childhood. He had early heard such songs as "Yargula" ("Yar" meaning "sweetheart" and "gula" meaning "colorful flowers"). The fact that *Argula* (Fig. 24), in the collection of the Museum of Modern Art, also belongs to this series suggests that he had combined memories of the folk song "Yargula" with the peasant rites fulfilled in this fabulous garden. In 1941 Gorky dictated the following notes and legend about the *Garden in Sochi*:[31]

"I like the heat, the tenderness, the edible, the lusciousness, the song of a single person, the bathtub full of water to bathe myself beneath the water. I like Uccello, Grünewald, Ingres, the drawings and sketches for paintings of Seurat, and that man Pablo Picasso.

"I measure all things by weight.

"I love my Mougouch. What about papa Cézanne! I hate things that are not like me and all the things I haven't got are God to me.

"Permit me—

"I like the wheatfields, the plough, the apricots, the shape of apricots, those flirts of the sun. And bread above all. . . .

"About 194 feet away from our house on the road to the spring, my father had a little garden with a few apple trees which had retired from giving fruit. There was a ground constantly in shade where grew incalculable amounts of wild carrots, and porcupines had made their nests. There was a blue rock half buried in the black earth with a few patches of moss placed here and there like fallen clouds. But from where came all the shadows in constant battle like the lancers of Paolo Uccello's painting? This garden was identified as the Garden of Wish Fulfillment and often I had seen my mother and other village women opening their bosoms and taking their soft and dependent breasts in their hands to rub them on the rock. Above all this stood an enormous tree all bleached under the sun, the rain, the cold, and deprived of leaves. This was the Holy Tree. I myself don't know why this tree was holy but I had witnessed many people, whoever did pass by, that would tear voluntarily a strip of their clothes and attach this to the tree. Thus through many years of the same act, like a veritable parade of banners under the pressure of wind all these personal inscriptions of signatures, very softly to my innocent ear used to give echo to the sh-h-h-sh-h of silver leaves of the poplars."

The earlier versions of this series used Miró as a catalytic agent but in subsequent ones Gorky gradually precipitated out more of his own thought. Similarly he eliminated traces of nature. A dual role was assigned to nature: it embraced the outside world seen by our eyes and the inside world of the psyche. Nature in this sense was to be transformed, abstracted and finally embodied in the disguised but nonetheless evocative form of symbols and images. In the earlier versions he illustrated the scene of the legend in detail: at the left of the canvas he boldly painted electric blue rock, black earth and flowerlike bits of multicolored cloth which pinwheeled from the top of a taut stem as though at the end of a child's kite string; then, in the middle, fancifully enlivened, the dark boot shape with a singing bird; and finally, on the right, placed the rollicking, curlicued shape of a crouched animal, probably a porcupine. But in the later versions the pictorial elements were absorbed more fully into the plastic body of the work. There was a new subtlety of rhythmic pattern, new freedom in the treatment of space and color. Space was now as real as the objects themselves; it appeared to come forward and recede, set in motion by the arabesque; it was used as labyrinth, or interior lake, and as enveloping mist; it might be still or palpitating. Color, too, was used suggestively rather than descriptively; it did not come up to the outline but rested within. *Tache* and line indicated the nature of the shape, but did not fix it unalterably.

In the black and possibly latest version (1942) there was still further interlocking and closing of spaces and weaving backward and forward from one shape or area to another so that, finally, this became the earliest example of the maze of the late period. Though Gorky had done the black to gray grisaille *Nighttime, Enigma and Nostalgia* (Fig. 15) in 1934,

24. Argula. 1938.

Oil. 15 x 24. Museum of Modern Art, gift of Bernard Davis.

67

25. Portrait. c. 1938.

Oil. 30¾ x 24¾. Estate of Arshile Gorky, courtesy Sidney Janis Gallery.

the black version of the *Garden in Sochi* was probably the earliest example of a predominantly black painting (where black was used as a color) in Gorky's work, or in the work of any American painter. (Highly interesting black paintings were to be done in the late forties and early fifties by Willem de Kooning, Franz Kline, Robert Motherwell, Clyfford Still and other painters of the modern movement.)

The *Garden in Sochi* series resumed many of the images and attitudes toward style of his earlier paintings. The red leaf shape, whose elliptical center is an eye, is familiar to us from a drawing of the 1932 period, as well as from *Painting* (Fig. 20, 1936-37). Inspired by an old-fashioned butter churn remembered from his childhood, the boot shape, first used in *Still Life* (Fig. 8, 1929), is the central image in all versions of the *Garden in Sochi*; and later may be seen in the *Anatomical Blackboard* (Fig. 39, 1943). The round shape of the orange version, seemingly so elementary, is on closer view seen to be composed of receding superimposed spheroids. The lower right-hand image is also closely allied to such paintings as *Personage, Battle at Sunset with the God of the Maize* (Fig. 22, 1936), and *Child of an Idumean Night* (Fig. 23, 1936), where the head becomes a sphere or perhaps in a play of metaphor merely an eye and the solid volumes of the human figure are compressed as in African sculpture. Also closely related is *Portrait* (Fig. 25, c. 1938).

In these paintings we are once more aware, as we had been in the *Still Life with Palette* (Fig. 9, 1930), and *Painting* (Fig. 20, 1936-37), of the use Gorky made of small and large spheres and ellipsoids. He needed points of emphasis; he needed stabilizing elements for structural purposes much as a carpenter would need joints and nails to hold his building firm. Gorky succeeded in giving a second meaning to these elements; they were not just plain nails but images as well. One might say that it was not fortunate coincidence alone that, just at that moment when he needed a nail for his structure, the appropriate image was at hand. Rather it was due to his ability to lift out of reality the shape needed—in other words, fertility in composing. He could always abstract or bring out of the thing seen elements which he needed for the thing he wished to make.

26. Garden in Sochi.
c. 1938-41.

Oil. 25 x 29. Estate of Arshile Gorky, courtesy Sidney Janis Gallery.

XI By 1935 Gorky's poverty forced him to the conclusion that his only chance to survive was to join the Federal Art Project of the WPA. His first project was to make designs for murals intended originally for Floyd Bennett Field, and later actually executed for the Newark Airport. Difficulty in eliminating a competitor came up and was settled in Gorky's favor by a jury composed of Audrey McMahon, Regional Director of the Federal Art Project, and Alfred Barr, the Director of the Museum of Modern Art. Mr. Barr, in casting his vote, had expressed the view that:

"... the Gorky project is better anyway from almost every point of view except a purely conventional or academic. I think the public would be much more interested in it than in the conventional allegories of [the other] project. I think too that the pilots and mechanicians would find Mr. Gorky's composition with its photomontage far livelier and more interesting."[32]

These murals, entitled "Aviation: Evolution of Forms under Aerodynamic Limitations," were to consist of ten large panels covering 1530 square feet (Figs. 30-33). Gorky's description of the murals, which he wrote for the WPA and which amounts to an aesthetic manifesto, says:

"The architectonic two-dimensional surface plane of walls must be retained in mural painting. How was I to overcome this plastic problem when the subject of my murals was that of the unbounded space of the sky-world of aviation? How keep the walls from flying away or else crushing together as they would be sure to do in a pictorial narrative? The problem resolved itself when I considered the new vision that flight has given to the eyes of man. The isle of Manhattan with all its skyscrapers from the view of an aeroplane five miles up becomes but a geographical map, a two-dimensional surface plane. This new perception simplifies the forms and shapes of earth objects. The thickness of objects is lost and only the space occupied by the objects remains. Such simplification removes all decorative details and leaves the artist with limitations which become a style, a plastic invention, particular to our time. How was I to utilize this new concept for my murals?

"In the popular idea or art, an aeroplane is painted as it might look in a photograph. But such a hackneyed concept has no architectural unity in the space that it is to occupy nor does it truthfully represent an aeroplane with all its ramifications. An operation was imperative, and that is why in the first panel of 'Activities on the Field' I had to dissect an aeroplane into its constituent parts. An aeroplane is composed of a variety of shapes and forms and I have used such elemental forms as a rudder, a wing, a wheel, a searchlight, etc., to create not only numerical interest, but also to include within a given wall space, plastic symbols of aviation. These plastic symbols are the permanent elements of aeroplanes that will not change with the change of design. These symbols, these forms, I have used in paralyzing disproportions in order to impress upon the spectator the miraculous new vision of our time. To add to the

intensity of these shapes, I have used such local colors as are to be seen on the aviation field, red, blue, yellow, black, gray, brown, because these colors were used originally to sharpen the objects against neutral backgrounds so that they could be seen clearly and quickly.

"The second panel of the same wall contains objects commonly used around a hangar, such as a ladder, a fire extinguisher, a gasoline truck, scales, etc. These objects I have dissected and reorganized in the same homogeneous arrangement as in the previous panel.

"In the panel 'Early Aviation,' I sought to bring into elemental terms the sensation of the passengers in the first balloon to the wonder of the sky around them and the earth beneath. Obviously this conception entails a different problem than those previously cited. In fact each of the walls presents a different problem concerning aviation and to solve each one, I had to use different concepts, different plastic qualities, different colors. Thus, to appreciate my panel of the first balloon, the spectator must seek to imaginatively enter into the miraculous sense of wonder experienced by the first balloonists. In the shock of surprise everything changes. The sky becomes green. The sun is black with astonishment on beholding an invention never before created by

29. Garden in Sochi Motif. 1942.

Oil. 16 x 20. Estate of Arshile Gorky, courtesy Sidney Janis Gallery.

73

the hand of God. And the earth is spotted with such elliptical brown forms as had never been seen before.

"This image of wonder I continued in the second panel. From the first balloon of Mongolfier, aviation developed until the wings of the modern aeroplane, figuratively speaking, stretch across the United States. The sky is still green for the wonders of the sky never cease, and the map of the United States takes on a new geographical outline because of the illusion of change brought about by the change in speed.

"The first three panels of 'Modern Aviation' contain the anatomical parts of autogyros in the process of soaring into space, and yet with the immobility of suspension. The fourth panel is a modern aeroplane simplified to its essential form and so spaced as to give a sense of flight.

"In the last three panels I have used arbitrary colors and shapes; the wing is black, the rudder yellow, so as to convey the sense that these modern gigantic

30. Aviation: Evolution of Forms under Aerodynamic Limitations. 1935-36.

Model showing four panels of the Newark Airport murals.

toys of men are decorated with the same fanciful play as children have in coloring their kites. In the same spirit the engine becomes in one place like the wings of a dragon and in another the wheels, propeller and motor take on the demonic speed of a meteor cleaving the atmosphere.

"In 'Mechanics of Flying' I have used morphic shapes. The objects portrayed, a thermometer, hygrometer, anemometer, an aeroplane map of the United States, all have a definitely important usage in aviation, and to emphasize this, I have given them importance by detaching them from their environment."

One may clearly see in the isolation of the wing removed from the body of a plane, for example, that Gorky was using the dislocation which was one of the cardinal theories of surrealism. At the same time, his semi-abstract use of machine forms and his decorative sense show affinities to Léger.

In an article by Frederick Kiesler published in 1936,[33] there is a very interesting pair of photographs. One is a photograph of a plane in flight,

74

31. Gorky Painting the Newark Airport Murals.

the other is a section of Gorky's mural. It is possible from this juxtaposition to understand how Gorky transplanted all parts of the airplane to the painting, including the naturalistic distortion of the camera shot. But (and here I disagree with Mr. Kiesler who says, ". . . it isn't abstract, but it looks like an abstraction") the omissions of links or parts, the will of the artist to place his object in a defined space, and to see this object as composed of a series of elements belonging to a plastic continuum rather than as a naturalistic event, has made of it an abstraction.

In one series of large studies, not actually carried out, Gorky employed, in the form of collage, photographs which Wyatt Davis had made of the elemental parts of the plane. He had long been familiar with Louis Aragon's "La Peinture au Défi," parts of which had been typed out for him by a friend. Various leading surrealist theorists had written in the following manner of collage—Tristan Tzara, for instance: "A form plucked from a newspaper and introduced in a drawing or picture incorporates a morsel of everyday reality into another reality constructed by the spirit." Louis Aragon, in "La Peinture au Défi": "Painters are now using objects as if they were words. Incantation has been invented again by the new magicians." Georges Hugnet: "The incorporation in a picture of an element foreign to painting reconciles the irreconcilable." And, "The public's reaction: 'This is not painting,' by itself proves the intense reality of the *papier collé,* the super-reality of collage."[34] Max Ernst had been among the first to use photographs in place of the pasted paper employed by the early cubists, but Ernst had used them only on a small scale. The use of photomontage in combination with mural painting was, so far as this writer knows, without precedent.

Gorky's model of the murals and one completed panel, exhibited at the Museum of Modern Art in 1936, caused much comment in the New Jersey newspapers. In answer to a request for his opinion on the murals Mr. Barr wrote:

"I am very much surprised to hear that there has been facetious and unfavorable publicity in the New Jersey papers regarding the murals for the Newark Airport, recently designed by the American painters Wyatt Davis and Gorky. I saw the studies for the murals and the recently completed scale models in the exhibition here in the Museum of Modern Art. I think they would form magnificent decorations of great appropriateness to an airport, for an airport should be one of the most modern architectural projects. Any conservative or banal or reactionary decorations would be extremely inappropriate. It is dangerous to ride in an old-fashioned airplane. It is inappropriate to wait and buy one's ticket surrounded by old-fashioned murals.

"One of the great mysteries of modern life is the enthusiasm for streamlined trains, automobiles and airplanes shown by people who at the same time are timid when confronted by equally modern painting.

32. Panel of the Newark Airport Murals. 1935-36.

Oil on canvas.

"I hope that Newark will take the lead in approving modern murals for a modern airport."[35]

Newark finally did, and the murals were installed. But only temporarily, and not without the further embarrassments and difficulties described by Stuart Davis:[36]

"I had one final contact with Gorky's work several years later. He had made some murals for the Federal Art Project which were allocated and temporarily installed in an airport in Newark, New Jersey. A local committee who had to approve them was hemming and hawing, and trying to find some valid excuse to reject them. It became necessary to smash this pesky rebellion, and the New York Project organized a delegation of overpowering authority to invade this benighted suburb and put the locals in their place. I was the artist member of the committee. We drove over the swamps in a determined mood and shortly met the stubborn and ill-armed locals face to face. There was nothing to it after the first broadside fired by our oratorical Professors, Doctors and Experts. One of the locals quickly joined our side, and the rout was complete. But their unhorsed chairman made a final convulsive effort by whistling for an ace pilot who charged into the room. "Tell these Yankees what you think of these so-called modernistic murals," the chairman gasped. The ace surveyed the huge pieces of canvas. They hung in drapery-like folds on the walls, owing to some slip-up in the secret formula of the adhesive which was guaranteed to last forever.[37] We all surveyed them; in spite of their orthodox hanging, they were unmistakably done in an approved modernistic style. But the chairman's ace-in-the-hole blasted his last hope by saying that he didn't know nothin' about art but thought they were right pretty. He said he was reminded of wonderful things he had seen, and began to recite recollections of beautiful cloud formations observed on his numerous flights. He was warming up to give dates, locations and the particular hour of the day of these events when the chairman silenced him. An official surrender was signed, and our cavalcade sped back victorious to the taverns of New York to celebrate."

Gorky did several more murals, including two very large compositions for the Aviation Building at the World's Fair in 1939, and a final set in 1941 for Ben Marden's Riviera night club on the New Jersey Palisades. Gorky was introduced to Ben Marden by Isamu Noguchi, and was given the job of decorating the great dining rotunda; as he informed Vartoosh, "I was to do a large mural." But apparently, due to the "war-created situation," Mr. Marden held off the actual completion of the work. Naturally, this was a great disappointment to Gorky, who needed the money. He fretted and complained to his sister, "I really worked hard on these pictures . . . slaving on them—then a few words are spoken and all my plans are upset." But, finally, Mr. Marden was able to let him go ahead and the murals were carried out.

All these murals show the same elements of architectonic unity, sym-

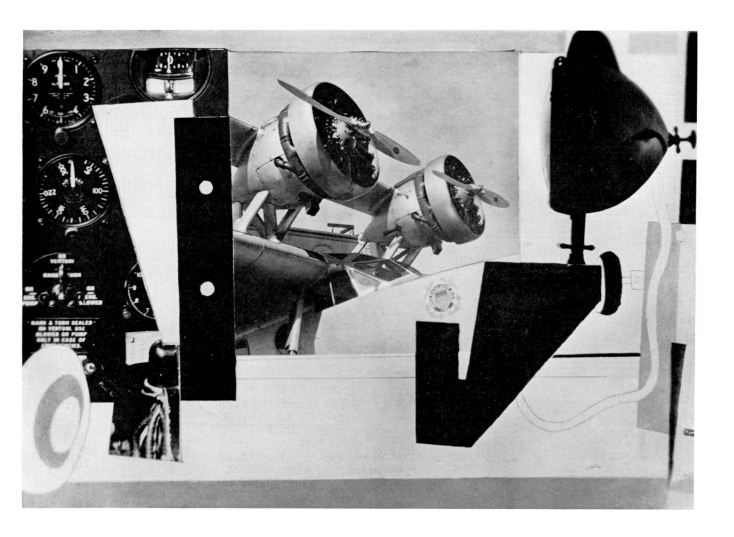

bolic use of essential forms and intellectual fantasy bordering at times on humor. Certain shapes and the light irony of some of the pictorial metaphors recall Miró. Of the Ben Marden murals Gorky said:

"I call these murals non-objective art, but if labels are needed this art may be termed surrealistic, although it functions as design and decoration. The murals have continuity of theme. The theme—visions of the sky and river. The coloring likewise is derived from this and the whole design is contrived to relate to the very architecture of the building.

"I might add that though the various forms all had specific meanings to me, it is the spectator's privilege to find his own meaning here. I feel that they will relate to or parallel mine.

"Of course the outward aspect of my murals seemingly does not relate to the average man's experience. But this is an illusion! What man has not stopped at twilight and on observing the distorted shape of his elongated shadow conjured up strange and moving and often fantastic fancies from it? Certainly we all dream and in this common denominator of everyone's experience I have been able to find a language for all to understand."[38]

33. Collage study for Newark Airport Murals. 1935-36.

Oil on canvas and photographs by Wyatt Davis.

79

Saul Schary worked at the Riviera at the same time on a smaller mural, entitled *The Rape of the Sabines.* This mural has been preserved, but the Gorky mural was "freshened up;" this "freshening up" was, unfortunately, so thorough that the original mural has been completely lost under the hand of some anonymous house painter. However, this job did serve the purpose of supplying Gorky with very necessary funds. His only other decorative project, a rug woven by V'Soske (Fig. 34), is now in the collection of the Museum of Modern Art.

A disastrous fate has overtaken all of Gorky's murals. Those at the Newark Airport, which were painted on canvas, have vanished, and all efforts to find them have failed so far. The World's Fair murals have disappeared, like most of the art made for the Fair. A few sketches and photographs are all that remains of Gorky's mural work.

34. Bull in the Sun. 1942.

7′ 5⅜″ x 10′. Rug designed by Gorky, executed by V'Soske. Museum of Modern Art, gift of Monroe Wheeler.

IV. Agony. 1947.

Oil. 40 x 50½. Museum of Modern Art, A. Conger Goodyear Fund.

Surrealism

I   Gorky had long suffered from poverty. From 1935-39, however, with the help of the WPA and the World's Fair job, things were somewhat better. He suffered less anxiety, managed to pay the rent, and now that he was earning over one hundred dollars a month he even paid a small income tax, token of a minimal security. But during the first years of the war, 1939-40, he was once more to know acute poverty. In fact, at the end of April 1940 Gorky wrote to Vartoosh, "The art business has not been so good this year—not a picture sold yet!" In September he tried without success to get a class going at the Grand Central School of Art, as we learn from a letter to Vartoosh:

"The other day," Gorky writes on September 3, 1940, "I went to see Mr. Greacen to ask if he would put a classroom . . . at my disposal. He said he would be glad to, but since there is a draft going on, he advised me to wait a few months, until he can tell more definitely how large an enrollment he would have. I can telephone him or call on him personally from time to time to keep abreast of developments. . . . In the meantime I shall place an ad in the paper announcing the opening of my school.[39] I earnestly wish that something would come of this effort, as life is becoming unbearable. . . . Do not worry about me, I'll get by somehow. Such is life and it is nothing new to me or to any other artist."

The war was, of course, occupying his mind. It was affecting him as an individual in his daily life, and as an artist. "This war," he wrote Vartoosh on December 28, 1941, "is assuming vast proportions. It seems I too shall be called to do camouflage painting. We artists are getting organized so that if called we shall serve as painters and not as soldiers." At this time Gorky applied to the draft board to serve in camouflage, but was rejected as past the draft age.

He then organized a course in camouflage at the Grand Central School of Art through the cooperation of Mr. Greacen, its director. For this course

81

he prepared with his usual eagerness, voraciously consuming all the literature on the subject, a literature which covered "data on protective coloring in zoology, optical illusions in the physics of light, and visual reactions to movement in Gestalt psychology."[40] The announcement given to prospective students contained a statement by Gorky as to the general aims of the course:

"An epidemic of destruction sweeps the world today. The mind of civilized man is set to stop it. What the enemy would destroy, however, he must first see. To confuse and paralyze this vision is the role of camouflage. Here the artist and more particularly the modern artist can fulfill a vital function for, opposed to this vision of destruction, is the vision of creation.

"Historically, it has been the artist's role to make manifest the beautiful inherent in all the objects of nature and man. In the study of the object, as a thing seen, he has acquired a profound understanding and sensibility concerning its visual aspects. The philosophy as well as the physical and psychological laws governing their relationships constitute the primary source material for the study of camouflage. The mastery of this visual intelligence has been the particular domain of the modern artist. Intent on the greatest exploration of the visible world it was the cubist painters who created the new magic of space and color that everywhere confronts our eyes in new architecture and design. Since then the various branches of modern art through exhaustive experiment and research have created a vast laboratory whose discoveries unveiled for all the secrets of form, line and color. For it is these elements that make an object visible and which are for the artist the vocabulary of his language.

"This course is dedicated to that artist, contemporary in his understanding of forces in the modern world, who would use this knowledge in a function of increasing importance. Such an artist will gain a knowledge that will deepen and enrich his understanding of art as well as make him an important contributor to civilian and military defense."

Gorky threw all his energies into this task, delivered several excellent lectures, constructed models and designs to demonstrate the principles of camouflage, and stimulated his students to make original contributions. But somehow the course bogged down. The venture was, unfortunately, not a success and had to be abandoned.

Though the United States' entry into the war affected Gorky deeply along with everyone else, his own personal and financial difficulties slowly began to ameliorate. It was indeed a crucial year for him.

Since 1937, when Juliana Force, then director, bought a painting for the Whitney Museum, no other major museum had purchased his work, though several had considered it of sufficient interest to show it repeatedly.

In 1941 the idea of presenting Gorky's work to the public by means of a gift to a museum came simultaneously to three of his friends, no one of them knowing that the other was taking this action; *Argula* (Fig. 24) was given to the Museum of Modern Art by Bernard Davis, one of the early collectors of Gorky's work; *Enigmatic Combat* (Fig. 21) to the San Francisco Museum by the mosaicist Jeanne Reynal; *Image in Xhorkom* (Fig. 19) to the Museum of Modern Art by Wolfgang S. Schwabacher; slightly later *Abstraction with Palette* was given to the Philadelphia Museum by Bernard Davis.[41] In the seven years remaining until Gorky's death in 1948 no further paintings were bought by museums or given to them. He did not receive a grant, though he tried for a Guggenheim Fellowship. He did not receive any prizes or mention at the large national or international exhibitions. With few exceptions no important collectors

35. The Pirate, II. 1943. Oil. 30 x 36. Collection of Julien Levy.

36. Drawing. 1943.

Pencil and crayon. 19⅞ x 27.
Sidney Janis Gallery.

acquired his work until after his death. He was not in demand as a lecturer, teacher, juror or committeeman. Little was written about him.

In comparison with other painters of his own generation and ability he was overlooked or by-passed, though the judgment of the art world since his death would seem to indicate that on the basis of quality his work deserved full recognition. Indeed it might be interesting to speculate what the result of less poverty and more success might have meant to Gorky. In any case it was not until 1945 that he could finally write to his sister Vartoosh, "This is the first year that I am working without any financial worries."

II Early in 1941 Gorky met Agnes Magruder, a young Bostonian in her early twenties, the daughter of an admiral, and fell in love with her. Agnes had bold, large blue eyes and jet black hair. There was a straightness about her, a something mysteriously alerted, springy, very beautiful. More important for his life, Gorky felt that she was fearless, while he, though strong, was full of fear, disaster-haunted, driven by inner and outer forces which crushed him, crushed the hard armor of his being as though it were wedged into a nutcracker.

From the first his pet name for Agnes was "Mougouch," a term of endearment in Armenia. It became one of her "aliases," as she described it. We will find in the following letter to her that the desire to have a center, to share a home was a deep instinct. Perhaps it was an instinct of self-preservation.

"My dearest love, I miss you terribly—this place seems so big without my Mougouch—and the telegram with it came the sad news—that you are ill—but why—you—having the measles—and your sweet letter—I have been praying to God—that it will be soon over—so that I might be with my Mougouch. . . .

"Cheer up Mougouch, dear, I am feeling well and looking after myself—I have provided myself with lots of vegetables and fruit. Most every morning I am up at 6 o'clock and take a bath, and walk in the park for an hour, and I am back to the house at 7, and work hard until seven o'clock in the evening. And at night I draw or look at the art books and dream about you—then I curse that measles. . . .

"Yesterday . . . I went to the zoo. The beasts had a curious effect on me, which I haven't hitherto experienced: I have always admired them, but now I hate them—the dreadful savagery of these wild animals who hurl themselves on their food is too horribly like the ways of humans. What moved me most was a group of four chimpanzees. They were like primitive man, they walked helping themselves with their hands, and looked like old men, their backs all bent, they discussed things in little groups, shared their food without dispute but with much wisdom—the strongest giving bread and carrots for the oranges and bananas belong-

37. Drawing. 1944.

Pencil and crayon. 19 x 23⅞.
Sidney Janis Gallery.

ing to the others. It's most depressing thus to see our own origin—depressing, not because we sprang from this, but that we may so easily slip back to it. Our knowledge is great, but how empty! How ephemeral! So small a thing, and we lose all. We no longer know chemistry as did the men of the Italian Renaissance, and it will be a long while before we rediscover their secrets. Art comes instinctively to us, but it is so uncertain. I have in front of me photographs of all Picasso's best works. The more I admire them the further I feel myself removed from all art, it seems so easy, so limited! We are part of the world creation, and we ourselves create nothing. Our knowledge allows us to make use of all the forces already in existence, our art to interpret emotions already felt. One big war, an epidemic, and we collapse into ignorance and darkness, fit sons of chimpanzees. Our one consolation is love, confidence, the embracing of spirit and body. When we are united we think neither of outer darkness nor of animal brutality. Our human superiority vibrates through our passions, and we love the world—but how insignificant we really are, and how subject to universal law! Mere midgets in the wide universe, but masters of our particular planet. Oh Mougouch, Mougouch, how strange it all is in my memory. I compare the slender springing grace of a lovely man with this hairy mass of monkey flesh—. The mastery of an energetic head, full of individual character, with the stupid mask of chimpanzees who can scarcely raise the beginnings of a smile. These comparisons are so terrible, so formidable in the mind; for if the blind masses of humanity, which always persecute their pioneer spirits, had the desire, or rather the power, then would our tall and erect stature be bent, and we should be covered with hideous fur, the grass would grow over our finest works, and we should return to bestiality.

"These wicked people who are so ignorant, we hate them—don't we, dear love? These brutes who have eyes for nothing save their animal passions, who think only of eating, who fight each other, and wallow in dirt—foul, disgusting fellows who only crush people of our kind, whose instinct is for beauty, for ideas, and for reflection, sweet dear. I am so blessed in being able to love you, blessed be the day when the great sun guided me to you. Without you, love, I should have been flung into an outer darkness, where bones rot, and where man is subject to the same law as beasts—final destruction, the humiliation of extinction. Dear, dear love, I press you to me with all my force, and only your help enables me to work. I thank you, dear fair lovely star, in having created women and men that we may be united, mingle our personalities, melt together our hearts and, by the union of our passionate bodies, better liberate our souls, making of us a single creature—the absolute human which you have endowed with so many gifts.

"Good-night, dear heart, sweet—sister, mother. Think that we are together in the same bed, and by our perfect union, making prayer to God."

Gorky went to San Francisco in the summer of 1941 on the promise of Jeanne Reynal to arrange an exhibition of his works in the San Francisco Museum of Art. The first days there he was uneasy about the various arrangements his friends were making and feared for the success of the venture. On August 4, 1941, however, he wrote Vartoosh, ". . . I believe everything is going to be all right. I have met many friends who in turn have introduced me to many others here, all helping me to succeed." Agnes was there; she had, through her parents, many acquaintances, and, as Gorky indicates, was working very hard to make his exhibit "a success." Now that he was in a happier mood he noted that "This city has beautiful scenes and a pleasant climate just like our homeland. The temperature reminds me of April and May." At last he was able to reassure Vartoosh, "Do not worry about us. Agnes is a very capable woman. Gradually, after knowing this city a little better, we shall be able to do better." He could tell her, too, that "Our friend, Miss Reynal, who purchased one of my pictures in New York," was there and doing her best to fulfill his hopes.

A few weeks later, on September 15, Gorky and Agnes were married in Virginia City, Nevada.

III Directly after their marriage Mougouch and Arshile came home to New York and 36 Union Square. The next year Agnes, expecting a baby, wrote to Vartoosh in October 1942 that they were sometimes "a little bewildered as to just what we will do with it once it is here." But as she explained hopefully, ". . . I am sure it will work out and Gorky is especially wonderful with babies and he had some practice with Karlen." (Karlen was Vartoosh's son and a great favorite of Gorky's.)

For the first time there was optimism in Gorky's letters to Vartoosh. "I am very happy," he wrote her on February 17, 1943. "Agnes takes good care of me, she's just wonderful." And he continued with further good news. "She is feeling fine." They had sold two more paintings which he hoped would "tide them over the next few months;" furthermore they were planning to go that summer to a farm of some 110 acres that Agnes' parents had acquired in Virginia—here he would do "some work on landscape provided, of course, that the place is sufficiently furnished for habitation. . . ." He adds the small but touching note, "We just had a telephone installed in our apartment, and Agnes is busy on it"—this was the first time he had had a telephone of his own. In this happy mood he longed to put the asceticism of the last years behind him and to amplify his life; he wished to have Agnes prepare for him the familiar dishes of his childhood, and he begged Vartoosh, "Will you write out in very plain letters the recipes for making Chelbour and also lentil soup as they used to make them back home?" As she had been ill, he added advice, "When summer comes," he wrote, "you must get a lot of sunshine; you must give the sun's rays a chance to work into your body. . . . Last summer Agnes and I spent two weeks outdoors, in the sun, and it worked wonders for us. This is the first cold I have had this winter, a light one, which will go away soon."

In April 1943 Agnes gave birth to a baby girl. They christened her Maro.

IV With the advent of surrealism art dared to move into man: man became its domain. It moved from the landscape to the mindscape, from the still life to dream life, from allegory to hallucination; in other words, away from what had hitherto been called the real. The layman became aware that he shared a common experience: the life of the unconscious, as it was vividly expressed in dreams. This experience was at once commonly shared and unique; each man dreamed but his dreams were uniquely his own. The surrealist accented these two aspects: the mythical quality of dreams, the perpetuation in them of the psychical history of the human race, and also their archaic and primitive residues in the individual. It was of enormous importance that men once more had a myth or form through which they could communicate, one that stood in real relationship to their experience. The need for art was no longer a matter of cultural compliance

38. The Liver is the Cock's Comb. 1943.

Pencil and crayon. 18⅝ x 24½. Collection of Julien Levy.

but of something more dynamic. It was for this reason that the surrealist appealed so deeply to our time.

We have seen how Gorky moved through the post-impressionism of Cézanne and the cubism of Braque, Juan Gris and Picasso toward surrealism. We have also seen how he moved from the near past of Cézanne to the near present of Picasso, and how, at this point, he reached back into the far past of Uccello and Piero della Francesca. While his passion for classical art continued he nonetheless successively interested himself in the work of men approaching ever closer to his own generation, experimenting with certain aspects of their ideas.

De Chirico had first made Gorky aware of the metaphysical beauties of the dream world; Miró had stimulated his desire to experiment in the direction of free fantasy and new concepts of space. By the end of the 1930's Gorky had assimilated those elements of cubism which interested him, and had virtually exhausted what he could get from Picasso. He now juxtaposed elements of different appearances or objects, bringing together things or bits of things which were actually widely separated and which were fused analogically for the first time by the inner compulsion of the artist in order to describe the world of the unconscious—the lost continent.

39. Anatomical Blackboard. 1943.

Pencil and crayon. 19⅞ x 27. Collection of Walter Bareiss.

These steps seemed to indicate full acceptance of surrealist possibilities. However, he was really in a different camp. While the surrealists, at least in the beginning, professed no conscious control of their unconscious material, Gorky was always in full control, aware of what he was doing and its meaning. He used the material of the unconscious with deliberate, conscious design. At this time his position was similar to that of Masson who said, ". . . I am too surrealist for those who do not like surrealism, and not surrealist enough for those who do."[42]

At this point I feel inclined to stress in detail what Gorky rejected in the work and attitudes of the surrealists. Pausing in meditation before his work and theirs I find myself reduced to negative terms, to describing what Gorky's work is not. He did not take surrealism or any modern isms over entire; they acted, rather, as modifying or catalytic agents. He was not an anarchist—that side of surrealism, for instance, coming down from dada, interested him but did not yield him anything. His work was not revolutionary in the sense of breaking sharply from the past. Gorky did not accept strict automatism nor did he rely on illusionary representation of fantasy or dream. He did not employ what Dali called the paranoid faculty for the double or triple image. His work was not haphazard, formless, alogical or contrived. It might be interesting to consider, too, what he did not

40. The Housatonic. 1943.

Ink and crayon. 19 x 24¾.
Collection of Mr. and Mrs.
Norton Simon.

41. The Plow and the Song.
1944.

Pencil and crayon. 19 x 25⅜.
The Allen Memorial Art
Museum, Oberlin College.

accept of the surrealist technical innovations. He did not, for instance, assimilate into his work the surrealist object as developed by Breton, in which
poetic writing adroitly supplements symbolic objects; nor the decalco-
mania-like effects or gyrating compositions of Max Ernst; nor the fusion
of techniques out of painting, *fumage* and photograph used by Matta, nor
the *trompe l'oeil* of Dali, nor the roto-reliefs, montages, paintings on glass,
and near objects of Marcel Duchamp; nor the collaborative composition of
J. T. Baargeld and Max Ernst; nor the compositions based on artificial accident of Arp and Dominguez; nor the fantastic machinery of Klee, Ernst
or Picabia.

V Gorky responded to life with the intense inner tremor of lyricism. The
charges of feeling stored up from innumerable experiences of past and present art increased the energy and acuteness of Gorky's response to the immediate outer world and sparked his creative imagination; but this quality of
exaltation was balanced by an opposite quality of calm reason; he filtered
his perceptions and analyzed both the world of appearances and the reasoned
methods by which he could recreate their essential aspect. Gorky's way
was a hard one, a way filled with the long, patient labor characteristic of
genius. He found abundant indications of his final and ideal style along this

way; and, as the momentum of his art accelerated, the sheer bulk of his processes heaved him out of himself, out of personal limitations, out of early
predilections, and left him free to record his own discoveries, which he was
now able to embody in fully rounded and perfected works that could
awaken thought, enlarge experience, and give delight. After more than
twenty years of grinding effort he was now, in the ripeness of his talents,
to achieve the supreme goal of an artist—communication.

In the prolific output of the next few years there was a new and height-
ened phase of lyricism, using landscape as a point of departure. Gorky was
primarily a poet and to him surrealism was chiefly valuable as a method
for releasing poetical inspiration. Fascinated equally by the "ineluctable
modality of the visible," in James Joyce's words, and the invisible, dark
work of the unconscious, he adopted an extremely rapid, semi-automatic
procedure, hoping in this way to catch thought at its quick, unhampered
by slow-moving logic. He left out links in the chain of thought, demanding
of the spectator a willingness to make a new effort of attention. His later
paintings may be better understood if we remember that he worked on several levels at once, responding to the stimuli of the immediate outside
world of nature, to anterior impressions of the Caucasus, to memories of
past and present art, and to the suggestions of the dream world or collective
unconscious. His art is evocative on four levels: the senses, the psyche, the
historic past and the universal level of epic symbolism.

Direct work before nature greatly broadened his vision. He now gave
full expression to his instinctive feeling for the morphology of living things.
He noted the mutations of form as well as the equally complex stream of
memory associations, and created hybrids which startle, reveal and satisfy.
In the work of the late period we find several main divisions: the calligraphic decorative, colored by an anthropomorphism similar to that of Picasso and Miró; the essential, the result of extreme condensation and reduction; the structural, in which he develops the morphology of forms
step by step, to the greatest possible "numerical interest," as Gorky said,
building a world; and themes based on a tragic poetry chiefly concerned
with the drama of sex.

The picture is now conceived as a system of relationships between
objects and space. The parts of objects are thrown out of their customary
propinquity, caused to function in a new way, to be seen separately, independently; they are then reorganized into a new synthesis where color
floats free of line and line carries the burden of depicting the image. Gorky's line finally conveys the image by means of a subtle movement which
expresses the metamorphoses of living things. There are paradoxes and
leaps as it defines aspects of the object, points out analogies and multiplies meanings.

Considering the ink drawings of 1929-32 (twenty-four on one theme alone!), then the many versions of *Battle at Sunset, Xhorkom* and the *Garden in Sochi*, we find that although Gorky needs to revise, condense, eliminate, recombine and perfect, he is increasingly able to shorten his toil by applying an original method to the highly differentiated material of nature. As he once explained to the writer, his method was to relate all distances between objects and himself to an imaginary point; he held a matchbox up before his eyes (literally, not figuratively) and to this fixed point he related the world in front of him, rather than to the horizon line. Cézanne once mentioned holding a piece of white paper before the eye to set off the colors in a landscape. Gorky, analogously, would establish his distances and spatial relations.

In 1942, a year after their marriage, the Gorkys spent three weeks in Saul Schary's home in Connecticut. Gorky had always felt a cold sense of isolation in the city, where he had been the exiled, alone among strangers. Nostalgically he had painted what he loved most—scenes of his earliest response to the beauty of the world. Now he worked outdoors. This experience was in the nature of a joyous shock of awakening. He reacted once more, as in his childhood, directly to nature; seen with the marvelous clarity of the invalid returned to health, the world was new, magical.

42. Good Afternoon Mrs. Lincoln. 1944.

Pencil and crayon. 19⅛ x 25¼. Collection of Julien Levy.

93

The Pirate, I, the first experience of this rebirth, was tender, tentative, trembling at the edge of new discoveries. The canvas was covered with subtly varied tones of green; the forms, somewhat in the style of lyrical cubism, were derived from flower and tree. Gorky's imagination drew metaphors from the shifting shapes of leaf formations spreading out or contracting in the breeze, much as Leonardo da Vinci had drawn battle scenes from spatterings of mud on an old wall. The *tache* or square patch used by Cézanne is employed here with greater breadth, and in the open space of Miró rather than in the closed space of Cézanne and Picasso.

In 1943 he followed this with *The Pirate, II* (Fig. 35), a study in contrast between partial emergence and partial obscurity, which shows the creator as he lives out the act of creating. We are made aware of the moment in which the artist lifts the veil; this is the moment of emergence. But he chooses not always to lift it but to permit at times a measure of obscurity which extends the range of suggestions. What is revealed in full clarity focuses our attention and satisfies our intellect; what remains unrevealed stirs the imagination and makes us yearn for the promised creation. Certain shapes of flower and leaf scarcely arise from the neutral gray-green of dawn; others are lifted into the yellow stream of early sunlight, and finally the upper right-hand flower is thrust into the rising light and its structure clearly analyzed. To the structure of space in a strictly formal sense a further dimension is added—the dimension of time, as the flower seems to grow. And in this way, painting is brought closer to music.

As Max Ernst has said, "A good jump requires a running start and one must go back to take it."[43] About 1938 Gorky had painted from nature a study of a waterfall which went back in style to his Cézanne phase of fifteen years before. Four or five years later he made the jump ahead—five years meant nothing to Gorky.

The *Waterfall* of 1942 keeps very close to the tinted drawing depending on calligraphy that rejects all natural appearance—elliptical, condensed and exquisitely plastic. The large *Waterfall* (Pl. II) of about 1943 expresses pure lyricism—the stream pouring between the rock walls lifts a fine spray over the yellow-lipped, pale, wet coral of the stone before losing itself in the opaque pool below. All around the living waters are magic greens lit by the imagination. There are affinities with the marvelous greens of El Greco. The horizon line at the top of the falls is high on the picture plane as in Japanese prints. Trees and foliage have become shapes drifted away from mere representation. Lyrical concentration has given way to hallucinatory images. In the midst of the powerful evocation of sunlight and the prolonged sound of falling water are the murmuring sounds of a spiritual waterfall—counterparts of the inner and outer world, the world of sensation and the world of imagination. Here the formation of images arises atavis-

43. Water of the Flowery Mill. 1944.

Oil. 42 x 48¾. The Metropolitan Museum of Art.

95

tically out of ancient memories; the concretion of these is the work of the imagination; the final depiction, uncritical but unerring, is the magical imprisonment of feeling and sensation in plastic and enduring form.

OPPOSITE:

V. The Betrothal, II. 1947.
Oil 50¾ x 38.

Whitney Museum of
American Art.

VI   As Gorky invariably drew careful studies preliminary to painting, it may be assumed that he made many drawings between 1933-43. There are, however, less than a handful from this period and we may only conjecture whether Gorky destroyed them, or whether they are in some private collection not yet known to the writer. A small group of transitional drawings, dated 1943, exists in which Gorky uses ink (as in 1929-32), but introduces crayon, as in the late drawings which were to follow. Though there is a certain stiffness in these first attempts to create new shapes as he sat directly before nature, especially when compared to the drawings of 1947 (only four years later), a sweet and sour effect intrigues us as the somewhat decorative quality of the over curved shapes is corrected by the bold, barbaric color of heavily applied crayon and the impact of the blacks.

In 1943 Agnes' parents were living in their newly acquired home, Crooked Run Farm, Hamilton, Virginia. That summer the Gorkys went to visit them for the first time, taking Maro along. Gorky was to love this place and to do some of his best work here. "It takes him," Agnes wrote, "a long time as a rule to feel at home—Virginia is one exception—it just touches something in him immediately."[44] She also noted that he was "fearfully linked with the sun"[45]—was this his Eastern heritage?—and that he worked best in the summer; this was always "his most fruitful time of the year."[46]

Here, working again from nature, Gorky went beyond the archaic quality of the transitional studies of the same year and created a series of lyrical explosions—scores of drawings in pencil and colored crayon. With their profusion of color, these mark his emergence into his mature style. As James Johnson Sweeney wrote shortly afterward: ". . . Gorky's latest work shows his realization of the value of literally returning to the earth . . . last summer Gorky decided to put out of his mind the galleries of Fifty-seventh Street and the reproductions of Picasso, Léger and Miró, and 'look into the grass,' as he put it. The product was a series of monumentally drawn details of what one might see in the heavy August grass, rendered without a thought of his fellow-artists' ambitions or theories of what a picture should be. And the result of this free response to nature was a freshness and personalization of idiom which Gorky had never previously approached, and a new vocabulary of forms on which he is at present drawing for a group of large oil paintings."[47]

The spectator might be inclined to see in these drawings only mor-

phological studies of natural organisms. It would be more pertinent, as André Breton pointed out, to see them as "hybrid forms."[48]

In certain of these drawings, such as Fig. 36, arching bridges composed of flower shapes top each other, curving over volumes of space; bridge upon bridge—and every bridge an image of flower clusters burst out of the grass into a new world. In Fig. 37 (done a year later) crystal shapes, not cut out of diamonds, but mobile, rise upward; one flame shape flickers in the whiteness; silver shadows tie in a curtain ring; a flower banner curves and blows in the wind; roots twist and spiral out of the earth; the thawed ground, in mute labor, gives forth diversity.

In these drawings (see also Figs. 38-40) we have observed that surface was, for Gorky, a very important means inseparable from color and line; a means further to define form and to suggest the enveloping atmosphere. He used many technical procedures; he rubbed down, washed or erased both pencil and crayon, permitting the accidental to suggest the ideal; where the heavily applied crayon dragged pencil dust with it he used this graying to neutralize tones which he considered too raw in their pure state. At times he etched the razored smoothness of the surface with a pencil, so sharp and so heavily driven as to tear the paper—how often I have seen the long lead of his pencil (sharpened to the length of a good inch beyond the wood) break under the pressure!

VII The Gorkys went to Virginia again in the spring of 1944 and stayed for nine months. Here Gorky made many drawings, (e.g., Figs. 41, 42) among them several for *The Plow and the Song*, one of his most beautiful 1947 paintings, and began many paintings that would, when finished, be dated 1945, the important opening year of his last period. It was a period of intensive work and one in which his invention seemed to be hitched to a star: remote, luminous, isolated.

Sitting before nature, Gorky dissected root, stem, insect, leaf and flower, studying genesis and process; out of these studies he created an alphabet of forms. As he worked he sang the plaintive melodies of the East—and with the song came moods and deep-sprung impressions whose haunting beauty infused mere analysis with emotion.

We may imagine that, confronted with the grass, he observed the fragile yet immutable spider-web design of nature, noting that if the design was the structure and foundation of the edifice, movement was life itself, not only in the sense of the tossed field, the swiftly moving bird or cloud, but in the transformations, in the action of life. The plants and the grasses seemed to grow beneath his eyes, and this process of growth toward fullness and the undercurl toward death fascinated him. He thought of flight,

97

concentrated on the image of flight as action, fecund, hedonistic; inherent, too, in the image of flight was the idea of voyage, escape, venture. Further, the stiff core of the waving pliant grasses interested him; he translated this stiffness as bone, contrasting the stasis of the bone with the metamorphosis of the leaf.

Master of translation, he created images that could overleap barriers of tradition and language differences. Frequently he himself symbolically indicates the barriers; he posts heavy and light ellipses—which appear as phantom presences—between the spectator and the world which he, as "fabulous artificer," creates; beyond this barrier, images disentangled from the mesh of outward appearances variously and provocatively repeat the sexual theme; in the boot shape, fetishistic symbol for woman; in flowers which suggest flight or imprecation; and in the cinglet, through which amoebic shapes push up to birth.

VIII Gorky's drawings of the summer of 1943 and later summers were the source for most of his later paintings. From now on, new developments in his imagery and even his style appeared first in his drawings, and were embodied in his paintings a year or so later. Often he squared off a drawing and transferred it to canvas, neither adding to nor subtracting from the original conception. It was a matter of concretizing ideas rather than creating them. Gorky considered a drawing as a plan or blueprint and followed its indication exactly. It is fascinating to observe how the forms of the drawing, translated into painting, took on body and weight.

In 1944 Gorky, working directly from the preceding summer's drawings, produced a series of paintings marked by a new wealth of imagery, freedom of handling and richness of color. Pushing to extremes in color sensation, he created arresting and frequently poignant parallels to extremes of mood. Boldly striking out toward new limits of experience, he permitted himself new liberties: a full-bodied, barbaric range of color, combined with somber, stabilizing, overpainted earths in *The Liver is the Cock's Comb* (Fig. 38, Pl. III); bleached, wave-washed rubbings in *Good Afternoon Mrs. Lincoln;* vibrant, transparent greens and reds in the *Water of the Flowery Mill* (Fig. 43) and *The Sun, the Dervish in the Tree.* The influence of Kandinsky may be felt in what seems to be a quality of improvisation, but in reality Gorky has followed completely worked out drawings in which the images are richer in texture and power of characterization than those of Kandinsky's earlier period and more flexible and plastic than Kandinsky's late geometrical paintings. These paintings which include also *The Leaf of the Artichoke is an Owl* (Fig. 44), have the fluid, amorphous, transparent quality of Matta, and at times Gorky, too, permitted his paint to

drip, using the resultant quality as a nuance of his thought; but, again, Gorky's structure is more mature, his shapes more plastic, and his cuisine more painterly and elegant. Gorky's own words for *The Liver is the Cock's Comb* were: "The song of a cardinal, liver, mirrors that have not caught reflection, the aggressively heraldic branches, the saliva of the hungry man whose face is painted with white chalk."[49] In this and other late paintings Gorky frequently used such primitive symbols as a man's body organs, the liver or viscera.

In *Good Afternoon Mrs. Lincoln* we find shapes molded with ancient-seeming colors—green, orange and yellow: these shapes, so like gestures, seem to emerge or recede, as waves of the spirit hurl themselves on the shore, pack sand into a gray smoothness, smother the sunlight, shape the stones in endless friction of sand and water. The images float in deep quietness suggesting the intimate poetry of helplessness at birth, unconscious wishes, words of a lost and ancient language, remembered only in dreams.

After these attempts to work out the problem of presenting crystallized images in an organized plastic space world and, simultaneously, through full color, Gorky turned temporarily to the opposite extreme. In a series

44. The Leaf of the Artichoke is an Owl. 1944.

Oil. 28 x 36. Collection of Mrs. Ethel K. Schwabacher.

99

45. Landscape Table. 1945.

Oil. 36 x 48. Collection of Mr. and Mrs. B. H. Friedman.

of paintings from 1944 to early 1946, he deliberately limited his objectives, working almost entirely in black and white and gray with a few notes of brilliant color. For the perfect flatness of white paper, the ideal two-dimensional plane, he substituted pure canvas, thus maintaining this ideal extension. The tones which he now applied sparingly were often transparent, no more than a breath, and cut into the virgin whiteness of the picture plane. Isolated shapes move in their own orbits; touches of color, elliptical *taches*, further activate space. They establish islands; these in turn are cut off by encircling areas. He isolates the separate words of his sentences and the letters of his words, and by deleting the connection lends them a peculiar importance—the importance of position. His meandering and rapid line is like the maze of Near Eastern and Persian calligraphy. If we follow it closely from left to right it may be seen to move over the whole canvas without ever coming to rest, one space invariably opening into another by however narrow a passage. It varies in thickness and emphasis, differing in this from Miró's line, which is singularly uniform. This liquid and rapidly moving black line of which Gorky was such a master attains the speed of a car moving down a macadam highway which meets no opposition from the road surface and is held back only by its own weight; Gorky's line meets little opposition in the picture plane, which is kept immaterial, as in a drawing. The speed of the drawing activates the space which is not cluttered with material presences. This speed affects us in much the same way as music; we apprehend it through its inner rhythm. Here line serves a double function: it is at once a reduction of an image or form and a line of communication between the divided worlds of the artist and the spectator. The artist sends a message over this line, the spectator receives it.

An important painting of this period, *Landscape Table* (Fig. 45), is particularly interesting. In it the line runs along and then there is a clog, landmark, or point, which is used as a measuring stage (related, as we have seen, to the matchbox before his eye); these points may become accents, color which give brightness, a feeling of the instant, of a discharge of force or energy; in another sense, the point is sometimes the center of a circle, the still center around which everything moves, or toward which things move; at other times the point is symbol for the smallest possible ellipse. The diminished ellipse is also a bar, a stake, an exclamation mark, an increased intensity. By allowing lines to lead off the canvas, Gorky is able to indicate that his space extends beyond the limited one of the picture plane; the whole landscape becomes a table—strangely, a dissecting table— where the chance meeting of flowers gives birth to symbols. If the whole landscape is a table, several of the images seem to be placed on individual tables. There is a feeling of individual still lifes, each on its own table, set

17713

101

up on a great table, the earth. Closely related in style is another painting of 1945, *The Unattainable* (Fig. 46).

The flowers that we find in *Child's Companion, Waterfall, Landscape Table, The Liver is the Cock's Comb, Anatomical Blackboard* and so many of his other late paintings and drawings are visionary—flowers of the mind setting forth the mind's story. The titles *Love of a New Gun, How My Mother's Embroidered Apron Unfolds in My Life* (Fig. 48), *The Backbone of My 1944 Ancestor Was Far Away*, are visionary, too, rather than realistic; they echo memories of the past, into which he probed deeply, and with which he builds, finally, in a manner not unlike that of Marcel Proust, whose seemingly rambling style is found to construct an enduring architecture.

IX   Many leading European artists of our time came to America just before and during the Second World War. In 1938, Jean Hélion; Yves Tanguy and Matta in 1939; in 1940 Dali, Fernand Léger and Mondrian; one year later the painters Max Ernst and André Masson, the poet André Breton and the sculptor Jacques Lipchitz; and in 1942 Marcel Duchamp returned. These artists did not entirely adapt themselves to the New York art world of the early 1940's nor did they contribute directly to the formation of our new art, but indirectly, through the influence of their personalities, they did affect our intellectual and spiritual climate.

Now that America was playing host to leading European artists Gorky found himself in a new relationship to authority. These were outstanding artists of his own age. Matta, born in 1912, was in fact of a later generation. Gorky was now released from the authority of the towering dead and the equally towering living. In his friendship with Tanguy and Matta he was to enjoy, at last, a reciprocal relationship—one in which mutual appreciation and criticism acted as a stimulus.

The Burliuks had been friends of Gorky for many years. An interesting painting done by David Burliuk, of a group of his and Gorky's mutual friends, Nicolai Cikovsky, Raphael and Moses Soyer, Mary Burliuk and the painter, presents Gorky's living head enigmatically as a bust on a marble pedestal. We may wonder whether this visionary portrait of Gorky was not an unconscious prophecy or tribute. Mary Burliuk has given authentic and interesting recollections of a meeting early in 1943 between Fernand Léger and Arshile Gorky in her article in *Color and Rhyme* for 1949:

"February 1943. It is 9 p.m. We are awaiting the arrival of Fernand Léger at Gorky's studio. . . . The guest is late. I look around. My attention is attracted by a red sofa of immense proportions, a red sofa with white pillows. . . ." Finally the guest arrives. "Arshile Gorky—thin, nervous, with his soft voice and enchanting laughter—looked overwhelmed with emotion.

46. The Unattainable. 1945.

Oil. 41⅛ x 29¼. Sidney Janis Gallery.

Fernand Léger was in his studio. Fernand Léger was his guest. . . . The great French artist walked into Gorky's kitchen. He is preparing steaks in French style. Léger is famous for his culinary gift. . . . The food is served and eaten. It is late now. Léger is on the giant sofa. He speaks. He speaks French only. . . . 'Now if you are not in the mood to show me your paintings—don't do it. One's heart belongs to his art and not always one can open his heart. But I would like for Agnes to tell me everything about Arshile's childhood. I want to know what made him feel that he must paint.'

". . . Agnes," Mary Burliuk continues, "began to translate her husband's quiet, deep, moving words.

" 'I remember myself when I was five years old. The year I first began to speak. Mother and I are going to church. We are there. For a while she left me standing before a painting. It was a painting of infernal regions. There were angels on the painting. White angels. And black angels. All the black angels were going to Hades. I looked at myself. I am black, too. It means there is no Heaven for me. A child's heart could not accept it. And I decided there and then to prove to the world that a black angel can be good, too, must be good and wants to give his inner goodness to the whole world, black and white world.' "

When, in the winter of 1944, Gorky accompanied Isamu Noguchi and Jeanne Reynal to a dinner given for André Breton at Margaret La Farge Osborn's, he had already heard of Breton as leader and animator of various groups, as a man who dominated his age and his friends, participated in numerous and ephemeral art magazines such as *V.V.V.*, protected and encouraged painters—and later excommunicated them when they differed from him.

Although they could not communicate directly, since Breton could not speak English, their liking for one another was strong and immediate. This was a period of upward and lyrical movement in Gorky's life. He had experienced the fulfillment of love in his marriage and in the birth of his first daughter, Maro. Now he was to experience friendship for his art, and for himself as an artist, through Breton (Fig. 47).

Many of the titles for his later paintings and drawings were invented by him in collaboration with Breton, Max Ernst and Julien Levy. It was customary for the surrealists to find titles for their works in the writings of poets and philosophers whom they admired. For example, *Diary of a Seducer* was suggested by Ernst from a chapter title in the great philosophical work *Either/Or* by Sören Kierkegaard.

The long succession of fathers Gorky found for his art (Picasso once said that in life it was a disgrace not to have a father, why in art was it a disgrace to have one?) were like his father, to be known only from a distance and never in the intimacy of exchange and development. They were to be known by hearsay, by their works, in the same way in which the old masters were known. Cézanne had his Pissarro, Picasso and Ingres their own fathers, Rimbaud his Izambard, but Gorky had to create his art-father just as he had to create his own father and to create himself and finally his art; he once said the way to keep painting was "to create something inside that makes you want to re-create it."[50] Upon meeting André Breton he had for the first time since his earliest childhood come upon the father in reality.

47. Gorky, Maro Gorky and André Breton, c. 1946.

X   For seven years Gorky had been without a gallery. Now that he had a family to support, however, he could not afford to risk free-lancing, so he decided to place his work once more with a dealer. As Julien Levy agreed to give him what seemed to be the most favorable terms, they signed a contract. This promised to be a fortunate relationship. Julien Levy was an astute and courageous dealer; in the early thirties he had shown the work of de Chirico, Dali, Giacometti, Tanguy and other avant-garde painters; he had also written a very lively work on surrealism. Their financial agreement was that Levy would guarantee Gorky $2,000 a year, and that in return he would receive twelve paintings and thirty drawings yearly. If Levy sold enough to repay himself the initial outlay, he would pay Gorky on the regular commission basis for anything further sold. Though $175 a month was scarcely adequate, it offered Gorky more security than he had ever had, and the hope that his situation would improve.

But Gorky's hopes in this direction were not to be realized. Julien Levy sold enough in the next years to cover the $2,000 stipend, but not more. According to Agnes' letters the financial relationship was not an easy one. Throughout the three years that Gorky was with Levy money matters were confused in nature, clouded by the latter's careless informality on the one hand, and on the other by Gorky's deep insecurity and—what one can call by no other name—timidity.

In March 1945, Julien Levy gave Arshile Gorky, then forty-one years old, a first important one-man show of his oil paintings in New York City. Just twenty years after he had first come to New York, he was, finally, to know a measure of success.

André Breton wrote a remarkable foreword to the catalogue from which I shall quote:[51]

". . . The eye-spring . . . Arshile Gorky—for me the first painter to whom the secret had been completely revealed! Truly the eye was not made to take inventory like an auctioneer, nor to flirt with delusions and false recognitions like a maniac. It was made to cast a lineament, a conducting wire between the most heterogeneous things. Such a wire, of maximum ductility, should allow us to understand, in a minimum of time, the relationships which connect, without possible discharge of continuity, innumerable physical and mental structures. These relationships have been scrambled interminably by false laws of conventional proximity (the apple calls for a pear in the fruit compote) or of scientific classification (for better or for worse the lobster and the spider are 'brothers' under the shell). The key of the mental prison can only be found in a break from such absurd manners of perception: the key lies in a free unlimited play of *analogies*.

"The register of analogies has been greatly extended and refined since the time when Fourier delighted in the discovery that a cabbage was the emblem

of mysterious love and foresaw the establishing of a color scale enabling us 'to know infallibly which passion is connected with what animal, vegetable, or mineral hieroglyph.' Rimbaud, Lautréamont and others have since travelled this road . . . but the primitive claim is still open and one can admire today a canvas signed by Gorky, 'The Liver is the Cock's Comb,' which should be considered the great open door to the analogy world.

"Easy-going amateurs will come here for their meager rewards: in spite of all warning to the contrary they will insist on seeing in these compositions a still life, a landscape, or a figure instead of daring to face the *hybrid* forms in which all human emotion is precipitated. . . .

48. How My Mother's Embroidered Apron Unfolds in My Life. 1944.

Oil. 40 x 45. Estate of Arshile Gorky, courtesy Sidney Janis Gallery.

107

"Here is an art entirely new, at the antipodes of those tendencies of today, fashion aiding confusion, which simulate surrealism by a limited and superficial counterfeit of its style. Here is the terminal of a most noble evolution, a most patient and rugged development which has been Gorky's for the past twenty years; the proof that only absolute purity of means in the service of unalterable freshness of impressions and the gift of unlimited effusion can empower a leap beyond the ordinary and the known to indicate, with an impeccable arrow of light, a real feeling of liberty."

That Gorky's inward satisfaction, at this time, was large we learn from a letter written to Vartoosh, July 4, 1945:

"I am enclosing a catalogue of my works on exhibit, Mr. André Breton wrote a review of my works. He is a world famous art critic, who writes about artists like Picasso.

"The exhibit was held at the Julien Levy Galleries, which usually houses rather serious works of art. All my paintings are to be shown at Julien Levy's this and probably the next year. Beyond that, we shall renew our contract if we agree on terms—that is how much he will pay me depending on the success my works will enjoy."

But Gorky's satisfaction was modified by the fact that there was little positive critical interest shown. The sponsorship of André Breton seemed to arouse antagonism, as we see from a review by Maude Riley in the *Art Digest*, March 15, 1945:

"Arshile Gorky . . . is painting incoherent 'accident' pictures (and don't try to deny this because a good percentage of the areas of his new paintings are running drips of turpentine), which it is said he paints in direct contact with nature. . . .

"Of what value is it to the artist or to ourselves, the untutored in sublimities, that Breton calls Gorky 'The Eye-Spring' and states that Gorky is 'for me the first painter to whom the secret has been completely revealed!' What's the secret? He doesn't say. Snobbery in the arts has surely reached its height!"

Even Clement Greenberg, who was shortly to become Gorky's most enthusiastic champion and the only American critic to write seriously and at length about him during his lifetime, was not favorably impressed by this first showing of Gorky's oil paintings. He found, on the contrary, that Gorky's present change "to the prismatic, iridescent color and open forms of abstract, 'biomorphic' surrealist painting . . . emphasizes the dependent nature of his inspiration" and commented that "Gorky has at last taken the easy way out—corrupted perhaps by the example of the worldly success of the imported surrealists. . . ." At the end of his review, he does note, however, a redeeming possibility.

". . . Gorky still continues to show promise! The most recently executed picture at this show, called 'They Will Take My Island' . . . indicates a partial return to serious painting and shows Gorky for the first time as almost completely original. It is not a strong picture and still makes concessions to charm, but it is a genuine contemporary work of art."[52]

XI   Gorky's friendships were intimately connected with his art; so far did it pervade his life that, as far as I know, he did not have any friends outside it, with the exception of his immediate family.

In later years Gorky's attitude toward my work was not such as it had been in 1934 and 1935 when I studied with him. From teacher he had become friend—and critic—as his way of looking at all work involved an attitude of instruction. He wished ceaselessly to learn and took it for granted that others did too. In the museum he would stop to give appreciation and advice to the copyists, or for the benefit of the visitor he would give an impromptu lecture, or would lend his rather saturnine attention to the museum lecturers, though he was skeptical of their merits and ready to discredit their assumptions.

As a critic Gorky always revealed something new, something unexpected, something I had never seen before, even in my own work. Faced with my painting he never said, "This is what I should have done," but made some suggestion that would lead to further thought and research. The object of his injunctions was to make me be myself in the greatest possible degree. He said to me once, very earnestly, "Find something you love, that is the important thing." And added, as illustration, "Mondrian's object, for instance, was the square—that is what he loved." After finding the object it was necessary only to pursue it to its final expression on the canvas—to realize it in essence and form.

For many years Gorky had thought deeply about the advantages and disadvantages of modern art. He had been drawn toward it and yet was not without conflict as he balanced the powerful attractions of the qualities inherent in the masterpieces of the past against those of the moderns. In a letter written May 31, 1941 to Agnes he writes of this struggle. As the letter is the only one known to the writer in which he discusses his ideas on art at any length, I will quote it entire:

"This morning after you left I was in the midst of arranging my drawings —and there were quantities spread all over the floor, Mr. Bernard Davis came in; he had hardly crossed the doorstep before he cried out, without ever stopping to wish me good morning or good day 'Hey! What are you doing? Walking over your drawings? There are mines of gold in them; how wasteful you are!'

109

. . . —then came in Noguchi—then we went to Metropolitan Museum of Art together. I looked particularly at all the primitive statues—Negro, Yellow, Red and White races, Gothic and Greeks, and I am glad to say I was at last convinced of a thing which had for a long time bothered me. I had never felt sure whether the very conventional form of the primitives, which gives only an enormous sensation of serene joy or exaggerated sorrow—always with a large movement, synthetized and directed toward one end—had not a comprehension more true, more one with nature: in other words, ampler and bigger, than modern sculpture from the Pisani through Donatello up to Rodin and the French of today. Having very carefully studied the true aspects, at the moment I think not. Up to what point I am absolutely justified I can't at all say. My first reason, and the one I consider most sound, is that primitive sculpture seen in large quantities bores me, whereas modern European sculpture seen in the same quantity interests me infinitely, without boring me, and if I go away from it it is because the strain of looking at it and understanding it upsets me, tires me, I have to go away, but with regret and with the firm intention to come back soon.

"All that seems to mean that I am an individual—Gorky—and it is my individual feeling which counts the most. Why? I do not know nor do I wish to know. I accept it as a fact which does not need explanation.

"Now, when I think it out I see that in modern sculpture the movement without being so big is nearer to the truth. Men do not move in one movement as with primitives: the movement is composed, and different parts of the body may move in opposed directions and with diverse speeds. Movement is the translation of life, and if art depicts life movement should come into art, since we are only aware of living because it moves. Our expressions belong to this same big movement and they show the most interesting aspects of the individual; his character, his personality. What kept me in doubt was, I think, the very simplicity of the early primitives in rendering movement, their conception of things in general being very simple, that of the modern being more complex. Today it all seems to me the other way around—the movement of the primitives is a misconception of true movement, is a fabrication of his mind, an automatic creation which corresponds in no way with the natural movement of living beings. In one word, it is complicated because he does not take the trouble to probe deeply, but invents, creates for himself. The movement of the modern seems to me to be simple because, putting aside all his natural capacity as a human automaton, he uses his energy to see well, in order to render well what he has felt well in seeing well. . . . To conclude, in order not to inflict Mougouch's ears too much, I am in entire sympathy with the modern European movement to the exclusion always of those moderns who belong to the other class, those who invent things instead of translating them."

As Gorky expressed his ideas in art most fully in his observations on the paintings in the museum, I will record my memories of one such visit.

110

I was painting flowers and Gorky had suggested looking at the rug in the Vermeer painting, *Allegory of the New Testament*, in the Metropolitan Museum. Some days later I met him accidentally in front of this very painting. He was standing there, intent, solitary, sad. The full view of Gorky's face was large scale, impressive, formidable. His black hair hung rather long and the back of his head was curiously flat. There was tenderness, cruelty and eagerness in his glance; he was communicative rather than responsive.

Hardly pausing to say "Hello," he pointed out the rug covered with a very dark black-green leaf design and occupying no more than two or three inches in the rather large painting. "Look at this," he remarked. "Delacroix spoke of the Greek coin being built from the center out. Vermeer has painted in this way, according to the principle of mass." He continued eagerly, "How beautifully they are drawn—Vermeer does not just make a leaf and place it in the design, he relates space and leaf."

At this point Gorky shifted his attention from the carpet, which he was showing me in order to help me solve my problem, to other parts of the painting and his own specific problems. "That drapery—it is abstract—observe how this shape" (he pointed to the ovoid space between shepherd and tree) "curves around the center space while the tree countercurves opposite it, cutting an egg shape such as Hans Arp loved to create, but not set off as Arp's was into a single work of art; Vermeer's shape is complete but one of many, it shines in pure singleness like one of a constellation of stars on a clear night." Gorky was totally absorbed, he went on in a low voice. "The spaces on the carpet that carry no configuration are, in fact, shapes of vital importance in building the whole." Talking half to himself, he continued to study the Vermeer. "Yes, Vermeer paints in thin layers—there is no waste effort—and those small dots—no, they are not like Seurat's, though they contain all the light the pointillist might have wished for, concentrated, hovering before the object, but not obliterating it." His analysis went on: "Vermeer is not a sun painter, but rather a moon painter—like Uccello—that is good, it is the pure, final stage of art, the moment when it becomes more real than reality." He paused thoughtfully. "One aspect," he continued, "of this super-reality is an extraordinary concentration on detail; see how he has drawn the snake so exactly with the red blood trickling onto the black and white diamond tiles of the floor. He has painted as Marianne Moore suggested a poet should write—'imaginary gardens with real toads.'"

We wandered on to the room of nineteenth-century French painting. As he talked Gorky drew close to a picture to absorb other vibrations than he had already noted through his eye; his hand moved forward with an

111

instinctive gesture as if he held a brush and was about to continue work. He turned alternately to me and then back to the painting as he spoke. An indefinable foreign accent softened the uncompromising tone of his voice as he continued persuasively in the method of question and answer. "It is true, is it not, that even Ingres had to revise—yes, the surface of the painting is smooth, finished and incorruptible as a diamond, but under the accomplished surface are *pentimenti*—see there at the shoulder, how the line of the black dress was lowered a fraction and the hand was extended to give greater elegance. . . . Are these not signs of the patient revision that even a genius has to make?" Gorky talked on, absorbed in what he was saying and quite unconscious of the impression he was making. He was fantastic yet reasonable, gentle yet fanatically obstinate, and burning with the conviction that art was important.

As we continued through the galleries Gorky, sweeping like some great bird fishing in the multitudinous waves, caught swiftly at provender: *Venus and the Luteplayer*.[53] "His apprentice must have done the head—it is too slick, Titian could never have been so vulgar." But the trees seen through the window, fronded, elegant as a peacock whose grass-green plumes fan with a rustling click in the spring: "That is Titian."

Gorky went down the great marble staircase, then wandered through the Egyptian room and the hall of medieval armor. He swooped again: two-inch Egyptian turquoise figurines: "Look how monumental they are, size is nothing;" Coptic embroideries: "Are they not better than Matisse—could he draw eyes blazing with such naked vitality?" In the armor room, surrounded by velvet and gold caparisoned horses, helmets, visors and spears, he exclaimed, "What shapes—I could spend a year studying them"—and as we returned to the main entrance he spoke of a Persian rug hung in the main hall: "How modern their conception of space was! They understood it in the seventeenth century; we are only just beginning to reunderstand it in the twentieth—see how they mesh the vines, the tendrils, the flowers with space and utilize these linked forms to create wholeness and radiance."

We were at the entrance. Here, inexhaustible, Gorky paused to look at postcards. He bought several.

XII "Gorky has just gotten some new drawing paper," Agnes wrote us from Connecticut in the summer of 1945, "and I see many canvases leaning against the studio in the sun—to whiten them you know. So there will follow at last some good days of work." And Vartoosh had similar news from Gorky:

VI. The Calendars. 1946-47.

Oil. 50 x 60. Private Collection, New York.

"It's good here and I am constantly working. . . . I did a lot of paintings and drawings [in Virginia] and all were well received in New York."

Later that summer we had news of another sort. Agnes, who had been carrying "what promises to be Gargantua himself," gave birth to a baby girl, and on August 31 she wrote us:

"We have another skirt! She was born August 8 and is the longest little one you ever saw. Gorky calls her his little pine tree, quite the best description of her, a straggling little pine with quite black hair and we call her Yalda."

A few days later the Gorkys decided to rename the baby Natasha.

The Gorkys had been living for the past nine months in David Hare's house in Roxbury, Connecticut. But on the tenth of September, 1945, they were moving in with friends, the architect Henry Hebbeln and his wife, who lived in nearby Sherman, until, as Agnes wrote, "the home they are fixing for us is finished—God knows that may not be till Christmas. . . . " Hebbeln was working on what later (actually not until 1947) became "the Glass House." At this juncture Agnes was worried about finding a studio for Gorky:

"Where Gorky will work in the interim is also a problem. . . . as you know Gorky's short view is always a dim one and at the moment he is cast down that we have to leave here. He is just working at a painting which he started when we first came out and which has been a great problem to him and at last he feels on the point of making, as they say of butter."

Her letter closed with a promise:

"We shall be in town now and again to shake the hayseeds from our hair and cut the hair too! Gorky's is down to his shoulders again and I shan't mention mine."

113

The Plow and the Song

I *The Plow and the Song* was the title of three of Gorky's late works (Pl. VIII, Fig. 67) and it seems a fitting title for the next-to-last period of his life. If the preceding five years had been richer and fuller of happiness than any that had gone before, the years 1946 and 1947 were the most productive.

As if he had a premonition that he had not long to live, Gorky was trying to compress into the short time remaining the work of a lifetime. "This summer," he wrote from Virginia, in 1946, "I finished a lot of drawings, 292 of them. Never have I been able to do so much work, and they are good, too." Often he painted all day and on until three or four o'clock in the morning. It was, as he confessed to Vartoosh, difficult— "Had I known that painting was so exhausting I should not have chosen it as a career. But, no matter, it must have been my destiny. I must have been born to it."

Since their return from Virginia at the end of November 1945 the Gorkys had been living with the Hebbelns in Sherman. Here Gorky had a studio in an old barn—which facilitated his strenuous if anxious preparations for his April exhibition at Julien Levy's. But in January 1946, just when he needed a calm interval of work, he was struck by the first in a series of three blows that led to the final disaster of his death. "Ten days ago," Gorky wrote to Vartoosh, February 5, 1946, "a fire starting in the chimney of my studio in Sherman, Conn., destroyed everything I had there: paintings, drawings, sketches, and books, all were burned to ashes, not a thing was salvaged. Well, it's too great a loss for me, and I don't wish to write about it any longer, as I don't want you to worry about it too. We are well and I am still working."

In detail the losses from the fire were, to quote Agnes, "Roughly at least 15 canvases painted in the year 1945, all the work of our 9 months in Roxbury and 3 months in Sherman, 2 excellent paintings of the Song and Plough theme, 3 or 4 portraits of me done over a period of 4 years and perhaps 6 paintings on which he worked intermittently for five or six years (realistic heads and flower paintings). The rest were along the lines of Jeanne's *They Will Take My Island.* . . . Anyhow the total loss in the fire was about 27 paintings.

After the fire Gorky came directly to New York. Fortunately friends were able to get him the loan of a penthouse studio for two months. Here he painted *Charred Beloved I* and *II* (Fig. 58) which, with the works he had already sent to Levy, barely made enough for a full show. This fact did not escape the notice of certain critics who commented on the few paintings in the exhibition, but failed to note that *Charred Beloved, Landscape Table* (Fig. 45), the *Diary of a Seducer* (Fig. 57) and *The Unattainable* (Fig. 46) were masterpieces.

II Late in February 1946, only a few weeks after the fire, Agnes came to me weeping. "Gorky is in Mt. Sinai Hospital. He will have to be operated on for cancer—will you come to see him?" As I sat next to his bed the day after the operation he spoke of the men on either side of him in the public ward; he was evidently touched by their patience in bearing pain.

49. Fireplace in Virginia. 1946.

Ink and crayon. 8½ x 10⅞. Estate of Arshile Gorky, courtesy Sidney Janis Gallery.

50. Fireplace in Virginia.
1946.

Ink and crayon. 8½ x 10⅞.
Estate of Arshile Gorky, courtesy
Sidney Janis Galley.

In front of him on the rolling bed-table was a Calder mobile lightly
trembling as footsteps passed by. There were flowers too. He told me
Agnes' aunt had sent a check, and Jeanne Reynal had sold securities to
give him a large sum outright; Serge Chermayeff had sent a round-robin
letter to the artists asking for help; my husband, Wolf Schwabacher, had
secured him a grant from a foundation and Mina Metzger the care of her
own physician, Dr. Harry Weiss.[54] This was true friendship such as he had
known in Erivan.

Nevertheless the tragic and downward movement of his life had begun. For Gorky, valuing health as a peasant does, this operation was a
traumatic experience, an attack on the integrity of his ego, a fatal impair-
ment of his physical completeness. But he was also a poet, and for the poet
it was a voyage—a quasi-mystical experience of the unknown.

III The Magruders vacationed in Canada in the summer of 1946 and the
Gorkys came once more to Crooked Run Farm, Hamilton, Virginia.

"We were like sick people," Agnes wrote from Hamilton, "when we
got down here. . . . We literally just lay on the grass for a week. Then
Gorky got up and started to draw as he hasn't been able to since we left here

116

51. Fireplace in Virginia.
1946.

Pencil and crayon. 19 x 25.
Sidney Janis Gallery.

2 summers ago—he already has a huge portfolio and he is so happy and well and beginning to want to paint," though under rather difficult conditions, for, as she adds, "The barn here burnt down last fall and he has no place to paint," but she hopes with a rather Spartan severity that, "when the urge really takes him he'll manage to paint anywhere." At any rate his heart was at peace here. So he went into the fields and made drawings all day long. By the end of the summer there were hundreds of drawings. Of these he wrote to Vartoosh, "I have never done better."

Gorky sang as inevitably as the lusty wood thrush—the song of the heart. While he sang we may suppose he concentrated on the problems he must solve. His distance to the object troubled him. At what point should he take his stand and establish his relationship to reality? At what level should he fix the horizon—low or high? Should he aim at clarity or mystery, the unveiling or veiling of form? He felt there was no hiatus in the linked thoughts leading to creation; before the work grew toward birth it was prenascent in the imagination. His gaze plunged into the bending feathered grasses, he even noted the inchworm on the leaf and the fascinating complexity of the angular, agile cricket. Each thing that moved across his spread of vision might alter the subtle balance of his seeing, his response to the endless intertwining of shape, the grading of hues, all the

117

vivid pageantry of the field; but self-inoculated against a sensibility grown burdensome, his mind held to the essential discovery of a new logic by means of which he could build an equivalent on the canvas of what he saw before him.

IV Gorky presented a vision which conveyed, in varying proportions, the main themes of love, death and fate, through a major image—the human figure; he expressed additional minor aspects appropriate to his thought through secondary images and symbols such as flowers, cradle, thorn, bird, beak, bone, chair, trellis; these he used as embellishments or as an elaboration of atmosphere and mood, not in the rarefied style of Matta. As Clement Greenberg pointed out, "Gorky owes something to Matta's drawing, but he has exalted this ingredient, developing it with a plenitude of painterly qualities such as Matta himself appears incapable of."[55]

In the firelit Magruder living room, the summer of 1946, he did a series of small drawings depicting interiors. Looked at casually they did not seem to deal directly with his major themes but they were, in fact, used as a base for some of his most important late paintings. He here introduced his major image—the human figure—and supplementary images of fire, receptacle and flight, developing them in varying combinations throughout the series. Figure 49 depicts a man extremely reduced, in the matchstick, concave-volume style of Giacometti. This man holds an enormous bouquet of flowers; on the table top to the right there is a large palette which floats as a free disk, dislocated from the legs which now become an independent shape; on the floor under the rocking chair at the far right is another palette. Man and chair alike are metaphorically identified with the bone to which they are reduced; the bone in turn is given the alternate shape of bird and thorned stem of a plant as variations of an essentially priapic image; chair, table and man are stems that support, boxes that contain. In Figure 50 the rocking chair and the fireplace with its tongue of flame are compressed into one image; between the legs of the rocking chair is, once more, a palette or further metaphor for the phallic principle. In Figure 51 the fireplace and rocking chair are present as well as a new image—the recumbent figure of a man. In Figures 52-53 there is a shape combining the idea of fire, receptacle and flight.

He did other drawings in the Virginia fields that were similarly based on his recent vision. At the upper left of a 1946 drawing (Fig. 55) leaves, each different in form, cluster momentarily above a shape which appears to be a double cradle; the lower cradle lying horizontally forms the base, the upper vertical cradle leans toward the apex of an understood pyramid. This extraordinary structure is composed of ovoid disk-like sections

118

and slender stalks. In the center image once again turret and cradle build into a triangle and at the upper right an inverted cradle, though it shelters the seed in the wind, seems to menace rather than protect. The point of view of the spectator shifts from the left, where he is looking directly at the objects, to the right, where he is looking up, in a perspective similar to that of a baroque ceiling. This is also true of a drawing (Fig. 54) where flying, catapulting, suspended shapes are scattered all over the basin of space; blades of grass become daggers, or spread like wings in flight; spatular shapes and disks are projected into motion; and flower forms surround apertures that yield further glimpses into the large basin which rounds in all directions as an inverted cup would to an eye placed somewhat below but at a centered point.

52. Fireplace in Virginia. c. 1946-47.

Ink and watercolor. 9¼ x 12½. Estate of Arshile Gorky, courtesy Sidney Janis Gallery.

53. Detail of Fireplace in Virginia (Fig. 52).

Of the culminating drawing of the 1946 period (Fig. 56) Gorky said, "This is a world." It was a world dominated by "the ghost of the unquiet father" inhabiting the person of André Breton, whose body was treated like an African or New Guinea fetish, the head equaling in size the stunted trunk which was represented by a hollow or negative volume. By the free use of double images he further emphasized the role of the secret progenitor (or father), the magic productive seed and the phallus by whose agency this world is brought into being.

V The Gorkys had lived in other people's houses since their marriage. They had never had their own home. But fortunately, in 1946, directly after Gorky's operation for cancer, Wolf Schwabacher secured a grant from the New Land Foundation which gave Gorky $1500 a year. The grant enabled Agnes to go forward with her idea of finding a permanent home. Agnes wrote to Wolf Schwabacher thanking him for this help. ". . . before I could answer such a lovely letter out of the sky drops Wolf with manna. . . . We are so very happy and feel so much nearer to our one big aim—a house . . . and the best way to show you how ardently thankful we are is to find such a house and do the work we know will come in such peace." She

120

promptly set out to find a place. "We did dash up to Conn.," Agnes wrote from Virginia, "for one week-end to hunt around Woodbury–Roxbury and we did find a really heavenly bucolic farm hideously expensive. . . ." Agnes longed to buy it, but the owners would not accept a lower figure, so she could only hope. "I am sure we can find something at our price, if we look long enough. But we must wait now until Gorky gets frozen in the fields or rather out of them. . . ." She could not interrupt him now for, as she knew, the summer was his most productive time. "He is working like a madman—a happy one. I tore 50 drawings away from him to send to Julien—it took him 2 whole days of muttering and puttering to make up his mind to send them and now he comes home exclaiming I must write to Julien to tell him they are nothing for only today he has discovered etc. etc. . . . Gorky says you must have one of these he is doing now, he will bring it to you when we come back." She found life with Gorky fascinating and alarming. "It is like riding a roller coaster, a huge dippy one to be sure but dizzy heights of elation that I can't describe for my heart is in my mouth."

In October Agnes communicated with Wolf Schwabacher about the house. ". . . I hesitate to show you my murky ideas on financing houses." She feared he would think her extravagant, and continued, rather defensively, "My only excuse is that I was more interested in liking something

54. Drawing. c. 1946.

Pencil and crayon. 17¾ x 23½.
Collection of Julien Levy.

than how I'd pay for it." She kept in touch with the real estate dealer in the hope of finding something more nearly her price, and finally exclaimed "which I had sort of thought was around $10,000—shocked!?" She was convinced Connecticut was the right spot for them; as she put it in her letter, "We have lived in Roxbury and know the people around there even unto the bank."

Later in October she wrote of her sadness at leaving Hamilton, "The days seem so short so suddenly and though we have loved every minute of it it's as though we must love these last days desperately. . . ."

Her letter to Wolf Schwabacher ended on a profoundly touching and hopeful note we did not often find in her correspondence, "It won't be long now before we shall have to leave here—Gorky drowns himself in work—work so sure and independent, so true that I feel quite shaken at times."

VI   Among the friends who occupied the studio at 36 Union Square during the periods when the Gorkys were in Connecticut or Virginia were Margaret Osborn, Serge Chermayeff and Jeanne Reynal. Late in the fall of 1946 Agnes wrote us, ". . . we are coming to New York next week and are hoping you will come and sup with us at the studio." However she was not sure of the exact day because, as she put it, "I never know just when we will be able to leave for it hinges on whether paint is dry." Actually they did come down a few days later and this supper turned out to be a party for Joan Miró.

We came to the party. Jeanne stood in the center of the room. Agnes was there too, very busy. And Gorky was in many places at once. He had scrubbed the floor that morning; it was immaculate. Many kinds of Armenian food were already laid out; everything had been ready for hours. As Agnes came out from the pantry alcove Gorky had built for her they moved forward together to welcome us. Gorky tall, and Agnes tall too, singular in her grace and youth. They introduced us to the others— Joan Miró, his friend, a Spanish architect, and Margaret La Farge Osborn.

After supper we sat about the enormous low table. Gorky offered wine in a bottle and without glasses. With reversed hand and arm bent sharply at the elbow he raised the flask to his lips, and tilting his head back, drank deeply from the curved spout. Then he passed the flask. No one could manage it, the wine spilled, faces were dripping, laughter mixed with the wine. Gaily Miró took the flask, sat straight, his legs firmly planted wide apart, then with a gesture of bravado and virtuosity, accomplished the feat. Waves of applause greeted him. Now there were requests

for song. Gorky sang the wailing trills and arpeggios of the East, songs of
Armenia and Georgian Russia, and Miró countered with Catalan songs,
close in spirit, high-keyed, ringing, intensely melancholy. Gorky answered
the request for dance with a few steps suited to the music.

55. Composition, II. 1946.

Pencil and crayon. 22¾ x 28¾.
Estate of Arshile Gorky, courtesy
Sidney Janis Gallery.

VII In the fall of 1946 Gorky was invited to participate, with eight
paintings and two drawings, in the exhibition "Fourteen Americans" at
the Museum of Modern Art.[56] This was the first large-scale official recognition Gorky had received in the East and was probably the definitive indication of a growing appreciation of his works. At the time, though he was
encouraged by the honor of being asked to exhibit in such an important
show, the success seemed inconclusive to Gorky, as it was not followed by
a warm response to his paintings from the general public. He told me he
thought that full recognition might well come only after his death as it

had with so many of the great artists who had been ahead of their time. Eventually, he felt, the public would accept these very paintings.

Soon after the opening at the Museum of Modern Art Gorky returned to Sherman. From there Agnes wrote that they were delighted with "Wolf's lovely letter with the totally unexpected windfall" and explained that they were going to get Gorky a new suit with it—"a much needed suit poor darling, his things are so out at the elbows people are convinced he affects it as a style." The letter continued with the news that "Gorky is much much better and were he not freezing in his studio—there's been a delay with the heat—we should be very happy indeed," especially as they found the "lakes, waterfalls, rocks and hemlocks around there so very beautiful."

VIII Gorky had identified himself with the most dynamic vision of our time in a long and arduous development. Now he was ready to achieve a synthesis of knowledge and creative power. In the next years he attained his full stature, which grew continually until the end. Fittingly, he was to express himself best as tragic poet. There had always been a deep undertone of tragedy in him and in his art, and perhaps his acutely sensitive mind was responding to the dominant creative mood of his generation.

In his *Lettres du voyant* Rimbaud wrote these lines, which Gorky loved: "The poet will define the amount of the unknown arising in his time in the universal soul; he will give more than the formula of his thought, more than the annotation of his march toward Progress! Enormity become norm, absorbed by everyone, he will be truly a multiplicator of progress!"[57] For Gorky the "amount of the unknown arising in his time" was the knowledge of the unconscious. He accepted the role of normalizer, finding new plastic forms to express discoveries made in underground labyrinths, and images to convey the enormous landscape of the uncharted world of the psyche. He no longer evoked this world in an autobiographical sense but as the universally sensed depth-ground of every man.

By now he had developed maximum technical flexibility and control and was ready to create his most complete and masterly works. Advancing from the simple to the complex, Gorky had evolved a final, highly original series of equations for his system of images and space. Now his aim was to give corporeal reality to his ideas; having found measurable equivalents for the signs in his equations, he sought to balance weight against weight within the limit of the work until it became a harmonious whole.

In this system space becomes pure extension: the image is balanced against emptiness which it invades, or disappears into. He obtains a wonderfully subtle and complex balance of volumes of space and ellipsoids, which seem to move upward against a surface tension that remains, or attempts to remain, at a dead calm. These paintings are studies in the control of objects and images, and the deceleration of their motions. The surface tension is so great that it seems difficult for submerged material to break through, or for the spectator to see down through the exterior. Nevertheless, the attentive imagination may respond to sequences of metaphor, symbol and allusion.

Dali's definition, "By a double image is meant such a representation of an object that it is also without the slightest physical or anatomical change, the representation of another entirely different object,"[58] was familiar to Gorky. But Gorky's double images, more closely related to the fantastic man-and-beast embodiments of Armenian illuminations, are formed of a condensation of two or more images—a technique noted by Freud in dreams. As Freud points out: "The process of condensation further explains certain constituents of the content of dreams which are peculiar to them and are not found in waking ideation. What I have

56. Drawing. 1946.
Pencil and crayon. 18½ x 24½. Whitney Museum of American Art, gift of Mr. and Mrs. Wolfgang S. Schwabacher.

in mind are 'collective' and 'composite figures' and the strange 'composite structures,' which are creations not unlike the composite animals invented by the folk-imagination of the Orient."[59] Gorky, by virtue of his Eastern heritage, was particularly endowed to create such "composite structures." He developed them, however, considerably further than his folk ancestors and in the direction of James Joyce's elaborate analogies. The parts of the original images surviving in the newly condensed image retain sufficient power to evoke all the images from which they are derived. This multiple-meaning image, whether word or shape, is an economical device, but one which makes unusual demands on the spectator.

A group of paintings which included *Diary of a Seducer* (Fig. 57, 1945), *Charred Beloved I* and *II* (Fig. 58, 1946) and *Nude* (Figs. 59-61, 1946) first fully embodied Gorky's final vision. This group was related in color to his black, white and gray paintings, but in richness of imagery and form it anticipated his final work.

These grisaille paintings and also several very large grisaille drawings in which he used charcoal, pastel, white chalk and crayon suggested at times the grace of Watteau. Gorky had admired enormously the Ingres *Odalisque en Grisaille* in the Metropolitan. Though in Ingres' time such a grisaille was considered as only a preparatory study for a full-colored painting, it had seemed to Gorky a finished work, to which it was not necessary to add color. Had not Picasso, also very much aware of Ingres' grisailles, done large paintings, including *Guernica*, in a black-to-gray tonality? In all this group, the mood was nocturnal, the painterly parallel to Rimbaud's line, *"Mes faims, c'est les bouts d'air noir."*[60] In a sense they were the final development of the essential mood of the ink drawings of 1932.

The *Diary of a Seducer* suggests the theme of the poet who sings to cheer his solitude. *Charred Beloved,* painted directly after the fire, suggests the traumatic quality of that experience; it might be called a reverie, out of which a film of smoke and flame awakens one, as if from a dream of disaster, to find that disaster has actually occurred. In *Nude,* bones—an image persistent among both painters and writers of the twentieth century—have the voluptuousness of flesh and seem more like two serpents feeding on each other in a subtle eroticism, whose softness is described by a line that becomes silent, expectant, veiled, waiting in extremity of tension for dissolution.

The desolation of these black-white wastelands is bitterly chilling. And yet, as always with Gorky, sadness is a means to intensify perception. Looking over the edge of the precipice into the abyss, he had learned the beauty of what he dreamt of losing forever. He now evokes a twilight or dawn world whose shapes descend through a mist of partial obscurity or

57. Diary of a Seducer. 1945.

Oil. 49¾ x 62. Collection of Mr. and Mrs. William A. M. Burden.

ascend nebulously to partial emergence. He evokes a deeper level of the psyche, the borderline world between waking and sleeping, teeming with latent images; on the universal level of epic symbolism, a world of life and death.

A group of some ten large paintings, most of them, like *Soft Night* (Fig. 62) and *The Limit* (Pl. VII), completed in 1947, represents a final synthesis of his art. Here he comes to grips with the main force of his basic themes, dramatizing, in an epic largeness of style, the tragic clash of human desire and fate. Each of these paintings stands by itself in mood and meaning; *Agony* (Fig. 63, Pl. IV) exemplifies dionysian passion and dramatic intensity; *The Orators* (Figs. 64, 65) intellectual fantasy and wit; *The Betrothal I* and *II* (Fig. 66, Pl. V) the appollonian qualities of perfection and elegance.

Most of this group are poetic expressions of a sex cycle. The idea content of dreams is recast and now flares up in a series of compelling visual images. *The Plow and the Song* (Pl. VIII, Figs. 41, 67) contains the theme of fertilization and birth; *The Betrothal* that of the wooing and drawing together of the sexes; *Agony* the battle of the sexes; *Dark Green Painting* (Fig. 68) a withdrawal into a hermetic world; and finally the *Last Painting* (Fig. 69) expresses the theme of despair and death. Gorky's world shifts between the drama of sadism, whose genealogy goes back to the writing of the Marquis de Sade, Baudelaire and Lautréamont, and the drama of occultism, whose genealogy goes back to Gérard de Nerval and Mallarmé. It shifts, in Nietzschean terms, between wild dionysian emotion and apollonian order.

In *The Plow and the Song* (Pl. VIII) we find the sun-warmed fertility of the earth, plow-turned; the sheltering bone, the winding birth passage and spacious exit chambers out of which the seed passes into space. The fields are a milky lemon ochre under a green-blue sky. The vertical image combines metaphors of plow, flower and bone, its base rooted in the moist field; its center is elaborated with suggestions of seed and leaf; its upper half, enveloped by the warm orange ochre earth, is raised in a pregnant gesture. The central image does not stand in vertical severity but lies semi-horizontally between field and sky; on the right the curving bone cleaves a wondrous ellipse, through which all life passes on its way to its destination; the final part of this image is the plow, poised, leaning ready to enter the earth, to till, to stir up the rich life within the ground. Themes of fertility are set forth here in various shapes and metaphors, celebrating a summer day in a field under the wide sky. Gorky's own words give us an added key to this painting. ". . . what I miss most are the songs in the fields. No one sings them any more. . . . And there are no more plows. I love a plow more than anything else on a farm."[61]

VII. The Limit. 1947.

Oil. 50¼ x 62¾. Estate of Arshile Gorky, courtesy Sidney Janis Gallery.

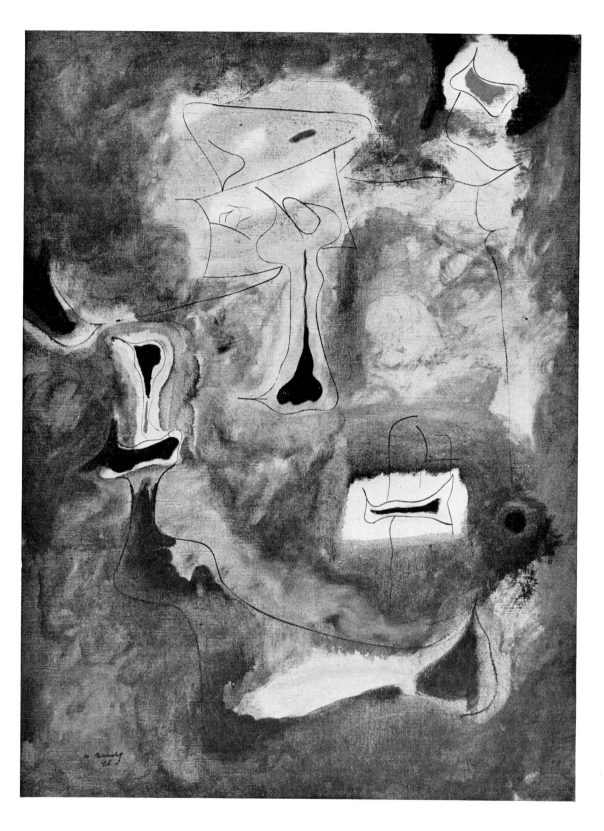

58. Charred Beloved, II. 1946.

Oil. 54 x 40. Martha Jackson Gallery.

59. Nude. 1946.

Ink. 9½ x 6¼. Estate of Arshile Gorky, courtesy Sidney Janis Gallery.

60. Detail of Nude (Fig. 59).

As early as 1924 Gorky had done a painting on the theme of horse and rider. In his studio at 36 Union Square he had placed on his wall nearly life-size photographs of Paolo Uccello's *Battle of San Romano* which he had contemplated incessantly. A small sketch of a prancing horse and rider, given by Gorky to Jeanne Reynal, was an exact copy of a detail from this painting. The thumbnail sketch was the germinal idea for Gorky's *Betrothal I* and *II* (Fig. 66, Pl. V). Without stretching the imagination too far one may sense allusions to the plumed helmet and spear of Paolo Uccello's riders. The images of horse and spear, or love and death are presented. The helmeted but featureless rider—Gorky often said, "I do not like to put a face on an image"—bestrides a phantom horse. The rider's body is traversed by a spear and so the betrothal takes on the meaning of Gorky's major theme, *Liebestod* or love-death. The voluptuous application of paint produces an atmosphere in which the rigor of what André Breton has called *"une courbe unique et absolument sûre"*[62] is more easily assimilated. The mellow milky ochre and honey tones, accented with lavender, pale yellow and red, enfold the opposing themes of love and death in poignant tenderness.

Black accents like gashes, rents in the curtain or surface of reality define a primary conception of a passageway; Gorky is obsessed with the relation of passage to portal; of the entrance way to the area or shape it enters, whether these are sexual orifices or portals to a larger body of discernible reality; we are everywhere led to consider the passageway—the gap between reality and reality.

Starting with dynamic and at times turgid studies, Gorky finally arrived at the graceful study for *Agony* (Fig. 63) and the rich dramatic quality of the painting *Agony* (Pl. IV) in the collection of the Museum of Modern Art. The series of drawings which are its basis center, as we have seen, around the fireplace in the Magruder home in Virginia. The fireplace itself and the other objects found in the drawings and the painting, such as the crib and rocking chair, appear to have been of the old-fashioned variety. But whatever they may have been actually, they are soon animated with Gorky's dreams; his ideas are presented as chains of images; his metaphors are linked. All objects in this room have one aspect in common. They are receptacles. The hearth comforts by its warmth, receiving and containing fire; the chair receives, lulls; by a shift of metaphor and emphasis, the hearth becomes woman in her receptive role. The flower petals denote her fertility. In this atmosphere of home, however, a drama takes place—the terrible struggle which gives its name to the painting. The fire now suggests immolation; and the mood is converted from contentment in the warmth and hospitality of woman to a heavier mood of fierce struggle.

131

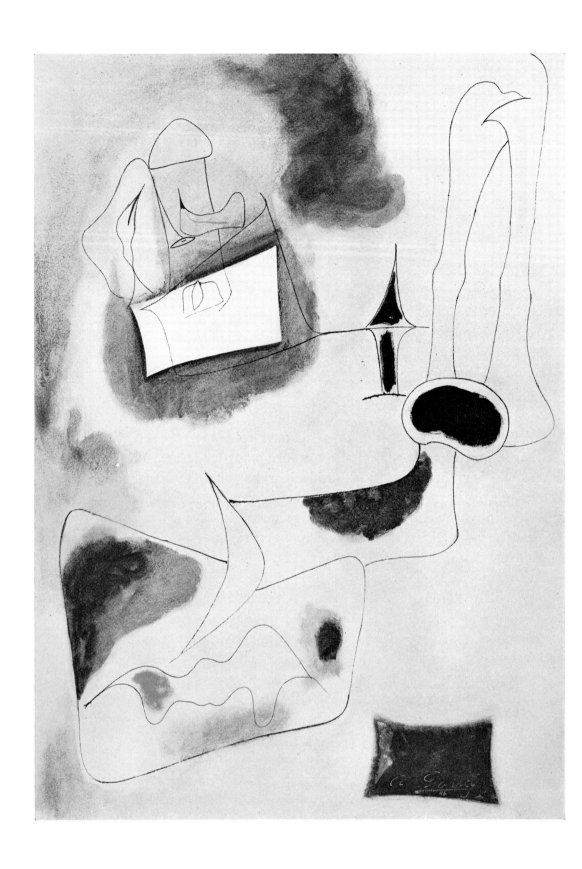

Gorky's use of the human figure may once more be seen in *The Orators* (Figs. 64, 65). In this powerful painting the central dominant group consists of an orator with expressively upraised hand and a lectern on which lies an open book. The full-length figure of a man laid out on a bier, a candle at his feet, lies straight across the canvas. Here, finally, the ghost of the unquiet father is laid with appropriate ceremony.

The summer of 1947 climaxed a year of the most intensive work—a peak year. Within its span Gorky turned out some three hundred drawings (of these eight or nine were really full-size cartoon studies for paintings) and some twenty oils. Depletion followed. By the fall he was exhausted, emotionally bankrupt.

OPPOSITE:

61. Nude. 1946.
Oil. 50 x 38⅛. Collection of Frederic Varady.

133

Agony

I Since the cancer operation in 1946, there had been increasingly serious personal conflicts which threatened Gorky's happiness and even his sanity. Though the operation had been a major one, it had not actually affected his sexual potency; but, due to the traumatic nature of the experience, he did, in effect, become temporarily impotent. And the tensions arising from this condition drove him into moody states of anxiety and anger. It is not possible to penetrate further into the emotions he was suffering, or to write down this tragic drama in full, but one can trace certain effects of these emotions on his life and their role in the final tragedy of his suicide.

At this eleventh hour and in the midst of Gorky's darkening mood and increased inability to work, critical approval and financial aid such as he had scarcely dared to dream of came his way. In the January 10, 1948, issue of *The Nation* Clement Greenberg, reviewing the Whitney Museum Annual Exhibition of Contemporary American Painting, finally wrote with full conviction: "Arshile Gorky's large 'The Calendars' [Pl. VI] is the best painting in the exhibition and one of the best pictures ever done by an American," though his enthusiasm was not unqualified. "True, it is an end product and begins nothing new in the history of art; yet it does seem to promise a series of masterpieces from at least this one painter—who has taken such a long time to arrive at himself, and whose chronic diffidence in the face of Parisian art has now at last been turned to full account."

Future critics will decide whether Gorky was an end product or an innovator or possibly both.

II Julien Levy was giving an exhibition of Gorky's painting in March 1948, so Agnes and Gorky came down from Sherman in time for the opening of the show. They stayed at Jeanne Reynal's. Their friends and hers dropped in to see them. She had a house on West Eleventh Street in the heart of Greenwich Village. There were paintings on every wall, paintings

62. Soft Night. 1947.

Oil. 37⅞ x 50. Collection of Mr. and Mrs. John Stephan.

63. Agony. c. 1946.

Pencil and crayon. 21½ x 29⅝.
Sidney Janis Gallery.

by Enrico Donati, Max Ernst, William Hayter, Wifredo Lam, Matta and, among the Americans, Jackson Pollock and Gorky. Hopi Indian dolls hung in clusters on the wall, and strange barbaric necklaces. Jeanne's studio, where she composed mosaics, was downstairs. Friends would come to dinner, which she cooked, and would stay to talk late into the night. Gorky was at home with the paintings, of course, but sophistication glanced off him; at heart he probably longed for the simple festivity of dance and song he had known in his childhood—wild, merry, raucous, innocent.

And as for surrealism he felt, as he sat there listening, that he did not care for it on its political side, nor even on its self-conscious intellectual side; that the preachment of non-logic and anarchy did not really appeal to him; and that what he liked in it was the poetry; after all, Louis Aragon, André Breton and Paul Eluard were poets, and the painters Arp, Dali and Ernst had poetic vision—this and their great technical skills gave their work importance.

III The 1948 exhibition at Julien Levy's was Gorky's fourth in as many years. It was to be his last. There the paintings hung—the field had yielded its song. Levy, quick, dark, subtle, willingly interpreted Gorky to

136

those who came to the opening—he had taken on the ungrateful task of providing a "Baedeker to a continent."[63] Many people milled around; their words drifted: "Too like Miró . . . obscure . . . extreme." Levy was accustomed to this state of mind in newcomers and paid scant attention to it. But gradually the confused state of the naïve spectators and the biting innuendoes of the acknowledged artists and critics must have overwhelmed Gorky.

When the Gorkys came to lunch with me the following day they seemed very dispirited, so, although it had never been my custom, in his presence, to say more about his work than "How beautiful," on this occasion I talked at length, speaking freely of my response to his painting. A day or so later, on March 2, Agnes, still very depressed, wrote me of this meeting:

64. The Orators. c. 1946.
Pencil and crayon. 19 x 24½.
Collection of Walter Bareiss.

"Ethel, you don't know how much it did our battered morale good to hear you talk about how you looked at Gorky's painting. We were just finding out how most people do it, even ones whom we thought didn't go symbol snatching and it was a rude shock to us both. I'm convinced there are still a few people above ground who love painting as painting not as a sop for gossip and pathology, and it is more of such people that Gorky should see."

Immediately after their visit with me they returned to Connecticut and sanctuary. Gorky was driven there, he felt, primarily by a failure of sympathy between himself and his audience. His depression was real but perhaps it was due partially to variability of mood and a certain impatience on his part. For it must be admitted that there was a swiftly growing appreciation of Gorky's work evident. Only a few days after his show opened, for instance, Clement Greenberg wrote the following enthusiastic review in the March 20 issue of *The Nation*:

"The presence of six pictures as excellent as those named above . . . declares a remarkable rate of performance, especially in view of the very high level the artist sets himself. And Gorky, in my opinion, has still to paint his greatest pictures. Meanwhile he is already the equal of any painter of his own generation anywhere."

IV Later in March the Gorkys visited New York again and I drove back with them to Connecticut through snow. We arrived in Sherman at night, stopped at the village store to pick up some groceries and then continued up the winding steep road to the Glass House which Hebbeln had built for them and which they had been renting, since they could not afford to buy it. Its windows reflected the night. We entered a spacious room all glass at one end. There was a mobile by Calder, a mosaic by Jeanne Reynal, a painting Gorky had purchased from my 1947 exhibition, and a drawing by Matta. Tall art books, a large couch and a fireplace, in which pine logs were soon burning, completed the setting. After dinner we sat around the fire for a short time looking at a catalogue of Giacometti. In the morning Gorky invited me into his studio, which was small and square, with a large north window. An old stove in the corner heated it and also dried the children's clothes. Gorky begged me to work. When I declined he showed me several of his paintings. Then he again asked me to work. He seemed to feel lonely, desperately in need of communication.

After a little we walked out into the icy world. Snow covered the rolling hills. We walked in back of Natasha, and as we walked Gorky smiled proudly. "She is a healthy girl. Look how solidly she plants her feet on the path." Then, as we trudged on, he pointed to the pine trees curving

65. The Orators. 1947.

Oil. 60 x 72. Collection of Mrs. H. Gates Lloyd.

down into the hollow slope: "Yes, it was this green that found its way into the painting, and the red-brown of the fallen pine-needles." As we looked at the white snow a strange breath of icy wind seemed to shake Gorky. I could not help feeling that the whiteness invaded him with a sense of emptiness and finality; now that the sun was sinking it was bitter cold. In the great living room of the Glass House the children Maro and Natasha were laughing and shouting. Gorky went in to them. Seating one on either knee, he gave them the toys he had brought from the city.

He painted only one more picture. Fittingly, *Last Painting* (Fig. 69) is pervaded by a sense of isolation which recalls Nietzsche's line, "Solitude has seven skins—nothing can penetrate it." This last work comes close to achieving Gorky's expressed desire to recapture the perfect identity of impulse and expression—to make painting as direct on the canvas as the emotion was within him. Like a scream in the night, it is violent, naked. A painting of raw emotion—non-art. At all points it touches the periphery of human feeling; it sings of the beyond.

V On June 26 Gorky's neck was broken in an automobile accident while he was driving in Connecticut with Muriel and Julien Levy. All three occupants of the car were rushed to the hospital in New Milford. Delirious, Gorky called for the doctor who had cared for him at the time of the cancer operation two and one-half years before. In quick response to his plea Mina Metzger and Dr. Harry Weiss drove up from New York. According to the doctors in the New Milford hospital and Dr. Weiss, Gorky had every reason to expect a full recovery from the purely physical effects of the broken vertebrae within a few months.

"Gorky is coming along," Agnes wrote us on June 29, "agonizing as the process is and I am constantly surprised at how well he looks with this incredible apparatus around his head and his enormous brown hands folded on his chest . . . but then of course he was in the pink of condition when this bit of luck caught him."

Agnes sifted the facts on the spot:

"It is fantastic," her letter continued, "that he is here now that I have visited the spot and reconstructed the plot! Actually it is a very dangerous hill . . . and as nearly as I can make out . . . they caught the hub of the wheel in the post marking a culvert on the side of the road and Gorky sitting on that side got the worst of it . . . darling Gorky is in hell just now though the doctor assures us it won't last. Tell that to Dante when you see this man on a hot night with . . . 2″ of flannel pad around his ears, chin and face drawn back by a 25 lb. weight. He no longer is plagued by horrible visions on the ceiling which nearly drove

66. The Betrothal, I. 1947.

Oil. 50¾ x 40. Collection of Martha Jackson.

him mad the first two days and he is regaining the use of his right hand so a great deal of torment has been allayed and he seems to be very comforted to just have me in the hospital near him which nearly breaks my heart as I am so conscious of my inability to share his pain. O well, it will be over soon and thank God it was no worse."

She planned ways to divert him during convalescence:

". . . it has occurred to me that the twelve weeks he has to spend in a collar will be less tedious if something very happy is going on around him and that would be a studio off from the house if we can get enough money from the insurance [payment after the accident] for that project I think Gorky would be terribly happy. So Wolf, I wanted to know if and how you would advise us. . . . I am so anxious not to seem to dump all our tedious problems in your far too kind laps yet we naturally turn to you as the wisest, most understanding one. . . ."

Agnes was ready to make every sacrifice to buy the Glass House, hoping that this would improve Gorky's state of mind:

"I am trying to sell my little house in Maine for the down payment on this one. I feel certain that that house will never be useful to us and I hope to get $5,000 for it. Bradbury [a local lawyer] is going to try and get the estate to take a $12-000 mortgage and we would have 94 and some odd dollars a month for 15 years plus taxes and insurance to pay for this house. That is what we pay now in rent and this way at least we will have something to show for it . . . and it will mean a lot to Gorky's state of mind and that is all that really counts so that actually the house will be worth more than the $16,800 we will be paying for it. Please my dear wise friends say you approve!"

We had several telephone conversations with Agnes as to whether this idea was wise and as to how it could be financed. My husband finally gave his approval.

Ten days later Gorky returned home from the hospital very much exhausted. He was broken by the heat and unable to sleep with his neck in a collar. Although he was beginning to regain the use of his right arm he still had to endure the frustration of not being able to work. And, most significantly, there were the deeply personal marital conflicts which, in his present state of dark depression, he could not hope to resolve. The rising fury of obsessive doubts and consuming jealousy that tormented him in the form of "horrible visions" as he lay brooding in the hospital now threatened to overwhelm him totally. A moving and illuminating letter that Agnes wrote us in 1949 helps to explain the swift development of the crisis toward disaster:

". . . it was a long struggle and possibly a wrong one before I realized that it was not one but three lives at stake. . . . Until the end I was still snatch-

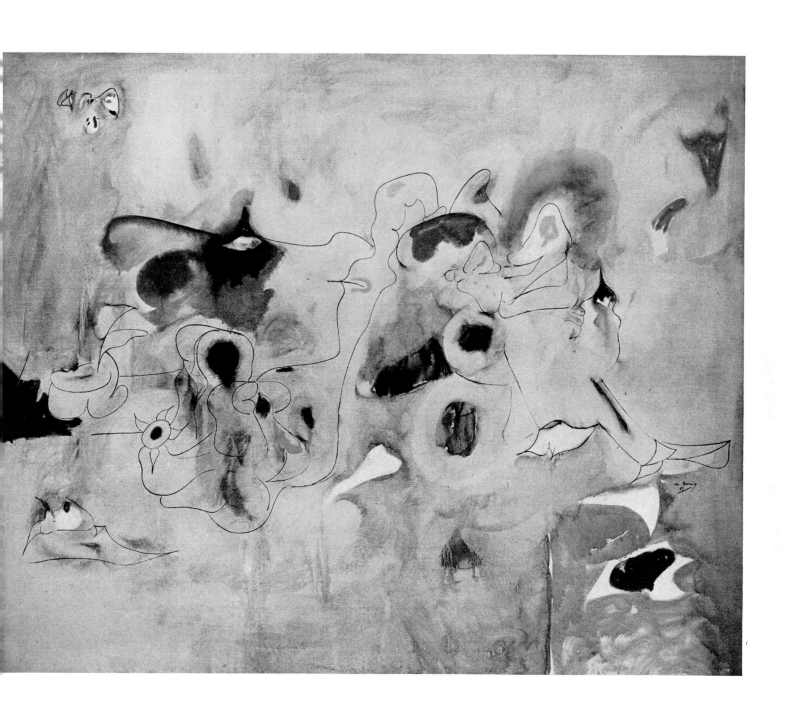

67. The Plow and the Song. 1947.

Oil. 50¾ x 62¾. The Allen Memorial Art Museum, Oberlin College.

ing at any straw that fell our way, money or a house, then a studio that would create the security he needed and relax his inner tension so that our problems could be solved more sanely and safely. The accident put an end to that effort, of that there can be no doubt . . . whether it would have failed anyway everyone but me seems to know. Perhaps I have said all these things to you before but can you hold it against me that I would seek again and again to show . . . that our life . . . was what it seemed to be, it was love and painting and roses and thorns and dark and light, all the things that get lost in a survey of facts and analysis."

Agnes left Connecticut, the Glass House and Gorky, and went with the children to her parents' home at Crooked Run Farm, Hamilton, Virginia. For Gorky the separation was a shock. The breaking of his home, like the breaking of his body, was insupportable. As poet, he had converted the experience of the operation into a quasi-mystical voyage into the unknown—a search for a phoenix-like rebirth; now blow after blow had brought him to spiritual exhaustion.

Gorky went to New York. There he stayed at Jeanne Reynal's home for the night. The following day he phoned us in Pennington in connection with the lease of the Connecticut house. In response to our invitation to visit us he said he would rather return to Connecticut, and added simply, "I am very unhappy. My home is broken up." We communicated with Mina Metzger who told us that Dr. Weiss had arranged for a psychiatrist to be called in who would see Gorky in three days' time, that Saul Schary was going with him to the Glass House and would stay for the weekend—and that we should not worry; Gorky was being taken care of.

The next morning, July 21, 1948, the day of Gorky's death, we received a letter from Agnes:

"I am sure," she wrote from Virginia, "by now you must have heard something from Gorky and whatever it was it must have been a great shock to you both. I am sorry that I myself can tell you nothing that will lighten your so kind and generous hearts—but only add to the drear weight of this final disaster. That it must be final I know not only from my own heart by now wrung quite bloodless but from the advice of Dr. Weiss. There is everything and nothing to explain. The words look so cold and short and it has been a very long and passionate struggle which I can no longer make especially as there are two hopeful little girls involved. Dr. Weiss is coldly objective though I know he has a warm understanding but he tells me from his standpoint the situation looks untenable and I *know* I can no longer hold on. . . .

"At the moment he [Gorky] is in no shape to make any decisions regarding the children nor do I know what we will be able to do with the future, even as to where we should live. I have written our tenant in the studio explaining the necessity of Gorky having it back—if for no other reason to try to establish

VIII. The Plow and the Song. 1947.

    Oil. 52 x 64. Collection of Mr. and Mrs. Milton A. Gordon.

a sense of continuity in his tormented world and later when I see how things go I must find a job and make a home for the girls. But as I say, Gorky is going through such a total turmoil that all plans are futile—I came down here without even a toothbrush on the advice of Dr. Weiss who warned me that this kind of situation can create the most serious psychic trauma in the life of a child and must be halted immediately. I think in a few days or a week I will take them up to Castine [Maine] until I can come to some understanding with Gorky.

"As to why I have never given you any inkling of what was going on I can only say that I thought the problem purely personal and a question of my adjusting to him and that I never conceived of life as easy and that if we failed it was because I had failed—a fatal case of inflation alas, for this thing is far beyond me now, and all his friends with all their warmth and affection can only help him if he can help himself.

"Believe me, my heart has been totally engaged even to the exclusion of my instinctive nature and if I could have I would have spared him this but my love was not strong enough I guess."

The sculptor, Isamu Noguchi, drove Gorky and Saul Schary back to Connecticut for the weekend. Dr. Weiss had prescribed sleeping pills. When Gorky returned to the Glass House he phoned Agnes in Virginia. She offered to come back to him. But he rang off abruptly.

The next day, as Schary started to leave, Gorky said, "Good-bye, Schary, do not worry. I am going to act as a man does." Schary was uneasy, but he said, "Good-bye, Gorky." Schary went to Peter Blume and his wife, who lived nearby, to tell them that Gorky was talking of committing suicide. Soon they heard from Kay Sage who had been alarmed by a telephone conversation with Gorky that morning. Peter Blume and his wife, accompanied by Malcolm Cowley, then went to talk to Gorky. It was too late. He had hanged himself.

And yet let us not be deceived by the tragic ending; this was a triumphant life—three hours packed into each one during its short span—and inordinately productive. This was a life that reached its goal.

145

Fame

When first I thought of writing about Gorky it was to bring him before the public and so help him gain the recognition he deserved. But Gorky no longer needs my help. His work has been circulated not only across the United States but also in Europe and in the Orient. Examples of his painting are now in many of the major museums and collections. In 1953 Henry McBride noted that the rooms of the Janis Gallery during the Gorky show were so crowded that he could see "but half a picture at a time," and that Mr. Janis informed him that half the pictures had already been sold and he thought seriously of advising the Gorky Estate to close the sale for the present; meaning, of course, that the pictures would bring more later. As McBride said, "Both kinds of success have been achieved for Gorky—the success of professional esteem and the final reward of a selling success."[64]

But more important for his lasting fame, there has come to Gorky the fervent admiration of the younger generation of painters who stood, as I personally witnessed, in rapt admiration before his paintings at the Whitney Museum Memorial Exhibition in 1951 and followed his work in the large show at the Princeton Museum in 1952 and in the smaller shows at the Kootz and Janis Galleries since then. Just as Gorky learned from his predecessors, the younger painters are now learning from him. It is not a question of passive imitation but of genuine influence. Perhaps they have caught something of his attitude toward the past and something, too, of his indomitable persistence in the search for his own truth. Gorky has been a civilizing, tradition-building influence and, paradoxically, an influence toward reaction from tradition. His painting and his personality have had the impact that is typical of genius.

During his life he suffered much from poverty. Perhaps a decidedly unpolitic and uncompromisingly frank way of expressing his opinions repelled many and held back his chance of success. Now that the thorns of his personality no longer prick, artists, critics and the official art world in general have had less difficulty in accepting Gorky and have placed him in

68. Dark Green Painting. c. 1948

Oil. 43¾ x 56. Estate of Arshile Gorky, courtesy Sidney Janis Gallery.

a position of unique importance. He has finally taken his rightful place as an old master of the modern school.

Some have felt that his art represented a culminating perfection of the trends that preceded it—that he was an end product—a modern Vermeer. Others have felt rather that he was an innovator and still others have seen in him a visionary. The force of his genius is apparent in this very fact. He is many things to many people, and is not to be easily defined or contained in a simple catchword. He created a world where all were invited to enter, to wander at will, to take from it what interested them—even to reject what did not. Gorky's world was inclusive: it contained much of the past —which he loved; it also contained much of the present. And finally it held within its spacious extent glimpses of the future.

69. Last Painting. 1948.

Oil. 30¾ x 39¾. Estate of Arshile Gorky, courtesy Sidney Janis Gallery.

NOTES

BIBLIOGRAPHY

INDEX

1. Agnes Gorky to Wolfgang and Ethel K. Schwabacher, May 1948.

2. Agnes Gorky Phillips to Ethel K. Schwabacher, December 1949.

3. Source unknown.

4. Arshile Gorky, "Stuart Davis," *Creative Art,* September 1931.

5. *Grand Central School of Art Quarterly,* November 1926.

6. For the facts of Gorky's early life I am indebted to his sisters, who have generously written their recollections for me.

7. Armenag Sakisian, "Notes on the Sculpture of the Church of Akhthamar," translated by Margaret Farrand Thorp, *Art Bulletin,* December 1943.

8. From an article by Gorky's nephew Karlen Mooradian, "Arshile Gorky," *Armenian Review,* Summer, 1955.

9. Vartoosh Mooradian to Ethel Schwabacher, February 8, 1955: "Our father always lived in Providence, R. I. When Gorky first came to the U.S. he saw our father for a short time. . . . A little more than a year after Gorky and I came to the U.S. our father remarried and because of this Gorky no longer associated with him."

10. Karlen Mooradian, *op. cit.*

11. Karlen Mooradian, *op. cit.*

12. Mrs. Edward M. Murphy to Elaine de Kooning, July 29, 1951.

13. New York *Post,* September 15, 1926.

14. For this chronology I have relied on Alfred H. Barr, Jr., ed., *Fantastic Art, Dada, Surrealism,* Museum of Modern Art, New York, 1936.

15. Peter Blanc, "The Artist and the Atom," *Magazine of Art,* April 1951.

16. To his sister Vartoosh, January 1, 1938.

17. Julien Levy, *Surrealism,* New York, 1936.

18. Mellon Galleries, Philadelphia, *Arshile Gorky,* exhibition catalogue, 1934.

19. *ibid.*

20. *ibid.*

21. A Greenwich Village restaurant.

22. Stuart Davis, "Arshile Gorky in the 1930's: A Personal Recollection," *Magazine of Art,* February 1951.

23. Arshile Gorky, *op. cit.*

24. André Breton, "Avis au lecteur," preface to Max Ernst, *La Femme 100 Têtes,* Paris, 1929.

25. To James Thrall Soby, March 15, 1951.

26. Hans Burkhardt to Ethel K. Schwabacher, May 1949.

27. Stuart Davis, *op. cit.*

28. From Paul Eluard, *Mourir de ne pas Mourir,* Paris, 1924, translated by Samuel Beckett, in Julien Levy, *op. cit.*

29. From André Breton and Paul Eluard, *L'Immaculée Conception,* Paris, 1930, translated by Samuel Beckett, in Julien Levy, *op. cit.*

30. In a letter to the author, 1954.

31. In 1941 the Museum of Modern Art had requested a description of the recently acquired *Garden in Sochi* for their files.

32. Alfred H. Barr, Jr., to Mrs. Audrey McMahon, December 3, 1935.

33. Frederick J. Kiesler, "Murals without Walls," *Art Front,* December 1936.

34. Georges Hugnet, "In the Light of Surrealism," translated by Margaret Scolari, in Alfred H. Barr, Jr., ed., *Fantastic Art, Dada, Surrealism,* Museum of Modern Art, New York, 1936.

35. Alfred H. Barr, Jr., to Miss Olive M. Lyford, Federal Art Project, October 14, 1936.

36. Stuart Davis, *op. cit.*

37. In a letter written to his sister Vartoosh in 1937 Gorky comments on this incident: "Dear ones, all those who are not American citizens will be dismissed from governmental work. That applies to me as well, since I have not got my second papers yet. However, since some of my pictures fell apart while being hung—which was not my fault at all, as others had applied the glue—I have to do those all over. And I hope by that time I shall have obtained my final papers."

38. Malcolm Johnson, "Cafe Life in New York," New York *Sun,* August 22, 1941.

39. The project of a school was never carried out.

40. Arshile Gorky, *Camouflage,* Grand Central School of Art, New York, 1942.

41. Received into the collection of the Museum of Modern Art: *Argula,* January 16, 1941; *Xhorkom,* April 7, 1941. This painting was exchanged for another version of *Xhorkom,* June 10, 1941, and finally, with the addition of a purchase fund, for the *Garden in Sochi,* on July 1, 1942.

42. "Eleven Europeans in America," *Museum of Modern Art Bulletin,* V. 13, nos. 4-5, 1946.

43. *ibid.*

44. Agnes Gorky to Wolfgang S. Schwabacher, October 1946.

45. Agnes Gorky to Ethel K. Schwabacher, June 1945.

46. Agnes Gorky to Wolfgang S. Schwabacher, August 1945.

47. James Johnson Sweeney, "Five American Painters," *Harper's Bazaar,* April 1944.

48. André Breton, "The Eye-Spring: Arshile Gorky," translated by Julien Levy, in Julien Levy Gallery, New York, *Arshile Gorky,* exhibition catalogue, 1945.

49. Quoted in Sidney Janis, *Abstract & Surrealist Art in America,* New York, 1944.

50. Talcott B. Clapp, "A Painter in a Glass House" [interview], Waterbury [Conn.] *Sunday Republican Magazine,* February 9, 1948.

51. André Breton, *op. cit.*

52. Clement Greenberg, *Nation,* March 24, 1945.

53. Many authorities now agree that this painting is a product of Titian's workshop.

54. Gorky gave Dr. Weiss two oil paintings in payment for his medical services. When I spoke to Dr. Weiss after Gorky's death he told me that at the time he accepted these paintings out of kindness in consideration of Gorky's poverty (not believing in their worth) but that later he had come to value them highly.

55. Clement Greenberg, *Nation,* March 20, 1948.

56. Organized by Dorothy C. Miller.

57. Jean-Arthur Rimbaud, *Prose Poems from the Illuminations,* translated by Louise Varèse, New York, 1946.

58. Salvador Dali, "The Stinking Ass," *This Quarter,* September 1932.

59. Sigmund Freud, *On Dreams,* translated by James Strachey, New York, 1952.

60. Jean-Arthur Rimbaud, "Fêtes de la Faim," *Oeuvres Complètes,* New York, n.d.

61. Talcott B. Clapp, *op. cit.*

62. André Breton, *Le Surréalisme et la Peinture,* New York, 1945.

63. Ezra Pound, "Henry James and Remy de Gourmont," *Make It New,* London, 1934.

64. "By Henry McBride," *Art News,* April 1953.

The place of publication is New York unless otherwise noted.

WRITINGS BY GORKY

Camouflage. Grand Central School of Art, 1942. [Announcement of Gorky's camouflage course.]

Stuart Davis. *Creative Art,* v. 9, Sept. 1931, p. 213-217.

General Description of Newark Airport Murals, c. 1936, 5 p. Unpublished. Copy at Whitney Museum.

Thirst. *Grand Central School of Art Quarterly,* Nov. 1926.

BOOKS

Baur, John I. H., ed.: *New Art in America,* Greenwich, Conn., 1957. "Arshile Gorky" by Lloyd Goodrich, p. 188-191. 4 il.

Baur, John I. H.: *Revolution and Tradition in Modern American Art,* Cambridge, 1951, p. 70-71. 1 il.

Blesh, Rudi: *Modern Art USA,* 1956, p. 132, 244-245, 257-259. 3 il.

Breton, André: *Le Surréalisme et la Peinture,* 1945, p. 196-199. 1 il.

——, *Young Cherry Trees Secured Against Hares,* 1946. Il. by Gorky.

Collection of the Société Anonyme, Yale University Art Gallery, New Haven, 1950, p. 34-35. 1 il. [Statement by George Heard Hamilton.]

Hess, Thomas B.: *Abstract Painting,* 1951, p. 5, 105-106, 108-111. 4 il.

Janis, Sidney: *Abstract & Surrealist Art in America,* 1944, p. 89, 120. 1 il.

Rodman, Selden: *The Eye of Man,* 1955, p. 122, 136, 137. 1 il.

EXHIBITION CATALOGUES

Hugo Gallery, New York: *Bloodflames,* 1947. [Includes "Arshile Gorky" by Nicolas Calas, p. 8. 1 il.]

Sidney Janis Gallery, New York: *Arshile Gorky in the Final Years,* 1953. 1 il.

Julien Levy Gallery, New York: *Arshile Gorky,* 1945. [Foreword, "The Eye-Spring: Arshile Gorky" by André Breton. Also included in Breton: Le Surréalisme et la Peinture, 1945.]

——, *Arshile Gorky,* 1948.

Kootz Gallery, New York: *Arshile Gorky,* 1950. 2 il. [Foreword by Adolph Gottlieb.]

Mellon Galleries, Philadelphia: *Arshile Gorky,* 1934. [Statements by Holger Cahill, Stuart Davis, F. J. Kiesler and Harriet Janowitz.]

Museum of Modern Art, N. Y.: *Abstract Painting and Sculpture in America,* by Andrew Carnduff Ritchie, 1951, p. 66, 126-127, 151. 2 il.

——, *An Exhibition of Work of 46 Painters & Sculptors under 35 Years of Age,* 1930.

——, *Fourteen Americans,* ed. by Dorothy C. Miller, 1946, p. 20-23. 4 il. [Quotes from "The Eye-Spring: Arshile Gorky" by André Breton, catalogue of Gorky exhibition, Julien Levy Gallery, 1945.]

Princeton University, The Art Museum: *Arshile Gorky,* 1952.

Bertha Schaefer Gallery, New York: *Hartley-Maurer,* 1950. [Statement by Hans Hofmann in "Homage to A. H. Maurer."]

Whitney Museum of American Art: *Abstract Painting in America,* 1935. 1 il.

——, *Arshile Gorky Memorial Exhibition,* 1951. 25 il. [Also shown at the Walker Art Center, Minneapolis, and the San Francisco Museum of Art, 1951.]

PERIODICALS

Balamuth, Lewis: I Met A. Gorky. *Color and Rhyme,* v. 19, 1949, p. 2-3.

Ballard, Louise: Art. *Arts & Architecture,* Los Angeles, v. 68, May 1951, p. 10-11.

Barr, Alfred H., Jr.: Gorky, de Kooning, Pollock. [In "7 Americans Open in Venice."] *Art News,* v. 49, Summer, 1950, p. 22, 60. 1 il.

Breuning, Margaret: A Memorial for Arshile Gorky. [In "Fifty-Seventh Street in Review."] *Art Digest,* v. 24, Apr. 1, 1950, p. 18. 1 il.

Burliuk, Mary: Arshile Gorky. *Color and Rhyme,* v. 19, 1949, p. 1-2. 5 il.

Clapp, Talcott B.: A Painter in a Glass House. Waterbury (Conn.) *Sunday Republican Magazine,* Feb. 9, 1948.

Coates, Robert M.: The Art Galleries. *New Yorker,* v. 21, Mar. 17, 1945, p. 77.

————, v. 26, Jan. 20, 1951, p. 60, 62-63.

————, v. 27, Feb. 28, 1953, p. 83.

Cowley, Malcolm: Arshile Gorky—A Note from a Friend. New York *Herald Tribune,* Sept. 5, 1948, Sec. 6, p. 3.

Curl, Huldah: Arshile Gorky Memorial Exhibition. Walker Art Center, Minneapolis, *Notes and Comments,* v. 5, Mar. 1951 [p. 1-2.] 1 il.

Davis, Stuart: Arshile Gorky in the 1930's: A Personal Recollection. *Magazine of Art,* v. 44, Feb. 1951, p. 56-58.

de Kooning, Elaine: Gorky: Painter of His Own Legend. *Art News,* v. 49, Jan. 1951, p. 38-41, 63-66. 10 il.

de Kooning, Willem. [Letter to the Editor.] *Art News,* v. 47, Jan. 1949, p. 6.

J. F.: Arshile Gorky. [In "Fifty-Seventh Street in Review."] *Art Digest,* v. 25, Feb. 1, 1951, p. 19.

Feinstein, Sam: A Gallery Itinerary. [In "Fortnight in Review."] *Art Digest,* v. 28, Apr. 15, 1954, p. 21.

Fetish of Antique Stifles Art Here, Says Gorky Kin. New York *Evening Post,* Sept. 15, 1926.

"Fiery River of Images." *Pictures on Exhibit,* v. 13, Jan. 1951, p. 4-5. 2 il.

Fitzsimmons, James: The Late Gorky. [In "57th Street."] *Art Digest,* v. 27, Mar. 1, 1953, p. 16.

Goodnough, Robert: Arshile Gorky. [In "Reviews and Previews."] *Art News,* v. 49, Feb. 1951, p. 46.

Goodrich, Lloyd: Notes on Eight Works by Arshile Gorky. *Magazine of Art,* v. 44, Feb. 1951, p. 59-61. 8 il.

Arshile Gorky Exhibits. *Art Digest,* v. 10, Jan. 1, 1936, p. 21.

Gorky: Was He Tops or Second Rate? *Art Digest,* v. 25, Jan. 15, 1951, p. 9, 30. 3 il.

Greenberg, Clement: Art. *Nation,* v. 160, Mar. 24, 1945, p. 342-343.

————, v. 162, May 4, 1946, p. 552-553.

————, v. 166, Jan. 10, 1948, p. 52.

————, v. 166, Mar. 20, 1948, p. 331-332.

————, v. 167, Dec. 11, 1948, p. 676.

————, Art Chronicle. *Partisan Review,* v. 15, Mar. 1948, p. 369. 2 il.

————, v. 17, May-June, 1950, p. 512, 513.

Hess, Thomas B.: Reviews & Previews. *Art News,* v. 49, Apr. 1950, p. 45. 1 il.

Johnson, Malcolm: Cafe Life in New York. [Gorky murals at Ben Marden's Riviera.] New York *Sun,* Aug. 22, 1941, p. 15.

Kees, Weldon: Art. *Nation,* v. 170, Apr. 8, 1950, p. 334.

Kiesler, Frederick J.: Murals without Walls: Relating to Gorky's Newark Project. *Art Front,* v. 2, Dec. 1936, p. 10-11. 2 il.

Kramer, Hilton: Month in Review. *Arts,* v. 30, Oct. 1955, p. 48-49. 2 il.

Krasne, Belle: Nine American Painters, Nine American Worlds. [In "New York."] *Art Digest,* v. 28, Jan. 15, 1954, p. 10-12. 1 il.

Lane, James W.: Current Exhibitions. *Parnassus,* v. 8, Mar. 1936, p. 27.

Lansford, Alonzo: Concentrated Doodles. *Art Digest,* v. 21, Mar. 1, 1947, p. 18.

Louchheim, Aline: Contemporary Art in New York. *Atlantic Monthly,* Boston, v. 186, Dec. 1950, p. 65-66.

McBride, Henry: Success at Last. [In "By Henry McBride."] *Art News,* v. 52, Apr. 1953, p. 66-67. 1 il.

Mooradian, Karlen: Arshile Gorky. *Armenian Review,* Boston, v. 8, Summer, 1955, p. 49-58. 4 il.

New York Exhibitions. *MKR's Art Outlook,* no. 11, June 1946, p. 7.

[Obituary] Arshile Gorky Dies. *Art Digest,* v. 22, Aug. 1, 1948, p. 27.

[Obituary] Arshile Gorky. *Art News,* v. 47, Sept. 1948, p. 56.

Old House Made New. *Life,* v. 24, Feb. 16, 1948, p. 90-92. 6 il.

Our Editorial. *Color and Rhyme,* v. 19, 1949, p. 1.

The Passing Shows. *Art News,* v. 44, Mar. 15, 1945, p. 24.

Porter, Fairfield: Arshile Gorky. [In "Reviews and Previews."] *Art News,* v. 53, Apr. 1954, p. 53.

————, v. 54, Nov. 1955, p. 50.

R. R.: Gorky, Matta, de Kooning, Pollock. [In "Month in Review."] *Arts Digest,* v. 29, June 1, 1955, p. 24.

Reed, Judith Kaye: Salvaged from Fire. *Art Digest,* v. 20, May 1, 1946, p. 13.

Reviews & Previews. *Art News,* v. 45, Apr. 1946, p. 54.

————, v. 46, Mar. 1947, p. 43.

————, v. 47, Mar. 1948, p. 46.

————, v. 47, Dec. 1948, p. 53-54. 1 il.

Riley, Maude: The Eye-Spring: Arshile Gorky. *Art Digest,* v. 19, Mar. 15, 1945, p. 10.

Seitz, William: A Gorky Exhibit. *Daily Princetonian,* v. 76, Oct. 14, 1952, p. 2.

————, Arshile Gorky's "The Plow and the Song." Oberlin College, *Allen Memorial Art Museum Bulletin*, v. 12, Fall 1954, p. 4-15. 5 il.

————, Spirit, Time and "Abstract Expressionism." *Magazine of Art*, v. 46, Feb. 1953, p. 82-84. 3 il.

Soby, James Thrall: Arshile Gorky. *Magazine of Art*, v. 44, Feb. 1951, p. 56. 1 il.

Sunley, Robert: Fourteen American Artists. *Critique*, v. 1, Oct. 1946, p. 21.

Sweeney, James Johnson: Five American Painters. *Harper's Bazaar*, v. 78, April 1944, p. 122, 124. 1 il.

————, L'art contemporain aux Etats-Unis. *Cahiers d'Art*, Paris, v. 13, no. 1-2, 1938, p. 51. 1 il.

Whitney Honors Gorky. *Art Digest*, v. 25, Jan. 1, 1951, p. 6.

LIBRARY
MODERN SERMONS
NATIONAL MUSEUM